Beyond th

MW01484663

The Metaphysics
of the Platonic Tradition

Ancient Writings on The One and the Gods

Selected and Introduced by Guy Wyndham-Jones

The Universe of Being
by
Tim Addey

A Prometheus Trust Students' Edition

The Prometheus Trust

The Prometheus Trust
14 Tylers Way
Sedbury
Chepstow
Gloucestershire
NP16 7AB, UK

Beyond the Shadows
The Metaphysics of the Platonic Tradition

Tim Addey

With writings from ancient authors
on The One and the Gods, selected
and introduced by Guy Wyndham-Jones

Second Edition 2011
(First Edition 2003)

ISBN 978 1898910 954

British Library Catalogue-in-Publication Data
A catalogue record for this book is
available from the British Library.

Printed in the UK by 4Edge Limited, Hockley

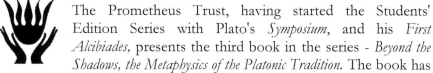 The Prometheus Trust, having started the Students' Edition Series with Plato's *Symposium*, and his *First Alcibiades*, presents the third book in the series - *Beyond the Shadows, the Metaphysics of the Platonic Tradition*. The book has two sections: in the first section a series of writings from the great authorities of the tradition on The One and the Gods is offered to the serious student of Platonic philosophy. These extracts bear repeated reading and meditation: they represent some of the most divinely inspired flights of human thought. The second section is a small work by Tim Addey which aims to provide a metaphysical framework for those who are beginning their studies in this profound philosophy.

The book is designed to follow the pattern by which the universe is produced: it starts with The One and the Gods, and unfolds the providential procession of their powers through the realms of being, in all its conditions. For this reason the first section requires the deepest thought, and we hope the reader will persist if at first its ideas seem obscure. It is probable that the newcomer will find it best to study the second section before working upon the first: but we are confident, however, that the lover of wisdom will treasure the writings of Plato, Plotinus, Proclus and Thomas Taylor and find in their splendid conceptions a never-failing source of inspiration.

It is noticeable how modern thinkers – as well as many university philosophy departments – shy away from examining pure metaphysics: indeed there is an (usually) unspoken thought that metaphysics is somehow unreal, or at least unreliable. But, of course, the underlying structures of reality cannot be ignored – they form the basis of our understanding of ethics, cosmology, epistemology, as well as many other areas of philosophic enquiry. The Platonic tradition sprang from a land which revered heroes – and the Platonic philosopher must, like Heracles, Theseus and Odysseus, set out bravely on the path of discovery, secure in the knowledge that Athene, Goddess of Wisdom and inspirer of heroes, is always close at hand, though perhaps unperceived. Although some of the concepts in this book are difficult because they are unfamiliar, nevertheless at heart they have a simplicity which, if we live with them for a while, will begin to cast a light within and around the philosophic soul – a light both beautiful and fair.

Contents

Platonic Philosophy – the Treasury without lock or guard

You might know, from the very entrance of the palace, that you beheld the splendid and pleasant residence of a God. For the lofty ceilings, which were curiously arched with citron-wood and ivory, were supported by golden pillars; and all the walls were ornamented, in every part, with silver carving, beasts of various kinds presenting themselves to the view, in the vestibule of the palace. Wonderful was the man, indeed, and endued with prodigious skill; or, rather, it was some demigod or God, who fashioned the silver carving with such exquisite subtility of art.

But the very pavement itself consisted of small shells, admirably decorated with pictures of various kinds. Blessed, thrice blessed, are those who tread on gems and bracelets! The other parts, too, of this wide-extended and regularly disposed palace were precious, beyond all price; and the walls being every where strengthened with bars of gold, were so refulgent with their own splendour, that, even in the absence of the sun, they made for the palace a day of its own; so bright were the bed-chambers, the porches, and the folding doors. The furniture, too, was answerable to the majesty of this abode; so that it might very properly be considered as a celestial palace, built by mighty Jupiter, for his correspondence with mankind.

Psyche, invited by the delightful aspect of the place, approached to it, and, assuming a little more confidence, entered within the threshold of the place. Presently after, being allured by the charms of the beautiful vision, every thing she surveyed filled her with admiration: and, in the more elevated part of the house, she beheld a magnificent repository, in which immense riches were contained. Indeed, there is not any thing in this universe with which this place is not replete. But amidst the admiration which such prodigious wealth excited, this was particularly wonderful, that this treasury of the whole world was not secured by any bars, or doors, or guards.

The Grove of
Academus

John D Quackenbos
1882

To Athena

Daughter of aegis-bearing Jove, divine,
Propitious to thy vot'ries prayer incline;
From thy great father's fount supremely bright,
Like fire resounding, leaping into light.
Shield-bearing goddess, hear, to whom belong
A manly mind, and power to tame the strong!
Oh, sprung from matchless might, with joyful mind
Accept this hymn; benevolent and kind!
Great goddess, hear! and on my dark'ned mind
Pour thy pure light in measure unconfin'd; -
That sacred light, O all-protecting queen,
Which beams eternal from thy face serene:
My soul, while wand'ring on the earth, inspire
With thy own blessed and impulsive fire;
And from thy fables, mystic and divine,
Give all her powers with holy light to shine.
Give love, give wisdom, and a power to love,
Incessant tending to the realms above;
Hear me, and save (for power is all thy own)
A soul desirous to be thine alone.

Proclus

Section One

Writings of the Platonic Philosophers

on

The One and the Gods

Selected and introduced

by

Guy Wyndham-Jones

The lyre of true philosophy is no less tuneful in the desert than in the city; and he who knows how to call forth its latent harmony in solitude, will not want the testimony of the multitude to convince him that its melody is ecstatic and divine.

Thomas Taylor

Writings on The One and the Gods

Introduction

"And let us as it were celebrate him, not as establishing the earth and the heavens, nor as giving subsistence to souls, and the generations of all animals; for he produced these indeed, but among the last of things; but, prior to these, let us celebrate him as unfolding into light the whole intelligible and intellectual genus of Gods, together with all the supermundane and mundane divinities - as the God of all Gods, the unity of all unities, and beyond the first adyta, - as more ineffable than all silence, and more unknown than all essence, - as holy among the holies, and concealed in the intelligible Gods."

Proclus, *Theology of Plato, II,*
xi

In introducing this little book, the reader should be aware that, in the first place, the subjects announced and investigated herein, though of the greatest and most profound importance, are so rarely discussed or touched upon by modern thinkers or theologians that they may appear to be not only novel and new, but also too vast to comprehend and assimilate. But in truth they are older than time itself, and are approachable and increasingly comprehensible by regular and frequent intellectual energy, which is in the heart of our nature and ours to harness and utilize at will.

All great challenges require consistent effort for their realization, especially in the early stages. So we should not be easily put off by the seeming immensity of the challenging vista presented in the following pieces, but rather, with concentrated votive power, we should gird ourselves for the beginning of a journey more worthwhile than any other for which we may strive, or desire, or make time for.

The Platonic panorama describes, as far as is humanly possible, the universal order of all things, beginning with that which is most simple and beyond all definition, through the generations of all beings, and terminating in the indefiniteness of matter and space. Its approach is truly philosophic, and scientific, and contains its own verification at every level - the verification of experience - as it is not knowledge that is the goal, but wisdom and union. For The One is beyond all science, the Gods are the causes of all science, and Being itself is the consummation of all science.

The greatest and most valuable jewel of the Platonic tradition is its theology, or teachings regarding The Gods, and their transcendent cause - The ONE. So sublime and fundamental is this theology, that without it all philosophy, religion, and science is but hollow and nebulous, without principle, order, or reason, leading only to cerebral knowledge, blind faith, and chaos. When once the true relationship of the soul to the Gods and to The One is glimpsed, which can only be as the result of inspiration, every thing, without exception, is transformed, and given a value not only appropriate to its nature, but a reason and cause at once both eternal and indestructible.

The idea of The One is the most simple state conceivable to the reasoning mind, and is approached not through addition or attribution, but through intelligent negation. For we must deny of The One anything and everything which compromises its simplicity. And in this is the profundity of Platonic thought revealed, as it removes every attribute from that which is alone and superessential (*i.e.* superior to being or essence), until we reach that state where words and thoughts and ideas are redundant. For whatever is added to The One lessens it, and dilutes its pre-eminent dignity.

Hence, The One is not the first god of many of the world's religions, as this god is complicated by and with its creations and even by the power which it possesses. Neither is The One omnipotent, omniscient, or omnipresent, as each of these conditions implies a power or energy or an essence in addition to unity. Neither is The One love, or truth, or the word, or made flesh, as all of these are attributes of that which is generated or revealed, and The One is beyond all generating power and revelation. But The One is so called because it is seen as that from which all things must proceed, and it is named The Good because it is to this all things desire to return - for all things and every thing desires good. Yet even these names do not fully indicate the exempt transcendence of this unknown nature.

In this process of removal, we should not worry that we shall be left with that which is empty, trifling, and omnideficient; for if it is love which directs this course, it will stimulate that which is most simple in us to unite with that which is most simple of all. This is beautifully expressed by Proclus when he says,[1] "Let us, by exciting the one which

---

[1] *Commentary on the Parmenides*, 1072.

we contain, and through this, causing the soul to revive, conjoin ourselves to The One itself, and establish ourselves in it as a port, standing above every thing intelligible in our nature, and dismissing every other energy, that we associate with it alone, and may, as it were, dance round it, abandoning those intellections of the soul which are employed about secondary concerns."

And that this is indeed not only possible for us, but also most desirable, is indicated by Proclus thus:[2] "I am of opinion, that the intellectual peculiarity of the soul is capable of apprehending intellectual forms (ideas), and the difference which subsists in them, but that the summit, and, as they say, the flower of intellect and hyparxis, is conjoined with the unities of beings, and through these, with the occult union of all the divine unities." That is, we are to be conjoined with the Gods, and through these, with The One.

It is well known that at the top of the highest mountains the air is thin and movement is difficult; and this is vastly more the case in our approach to The One, when words, thoughts, ideas, energies, and powers are left behind, and, breathless and still, we are absorbed alone with the alone. It is an experience that words may indicate but cannot really describe. But it is nevertheless more real than all love, joy, and bliss rolled in one, multiplied, and enjoyed together and at once - and can never be forgotten or denied. The reader must consider the profundity of The One for himself or herself in the deepest reaches of their being, and, with silent attention and awe-full expectation, the presence of The One may be perceived.

The One is superessential, simply and only; but the Gods are superessential whilst generating all essence, power, and energy, all being, life, and intelligence, and all goodness, wisdom, and beauty. For unity is supplied to all things from The One, but the Gods fill all things, by their very presence, with everything that is essential, vital, intelligible, and permanent. This presence of the Gods is so very intimate with our nature that it is rarely perceived as being with us or in us, except when the best part of us is in energy and directs itself to the heart of our being.

If The One is unity, then the Gods are ones or unities. But they are not attributes or elements, or qualities of The One, for if they were, The One would be many and void of its indescribable simplicity. In the words of Thomas Taylor: "Self-subsistent superessential natures are

---

[2] *Theology of Plato*, I, 3.

the immediate progeny of The One, if it be lawful thus to denominate things which ought rather to be called ineffable unfoldings into light from the ineffable; for progeny implies a producing cause, and The One must be conceived as something even more excellent than this. From this divine self-perfect and self-producing multitude, a series of self-perfect natures, *viz.* of beings, lives, intellects, and souls proceeds, according to Plato, in the last link of which luminous series he also classes the human soul, proximately suspended from the order of daemons; for this order, as he clearly asserts in the *Banquet*, stands in the middle rank between the divine and the human, fills up the vacant space, and links together all intelligent nature."

The Gods are, so to speak, the key to reality, the basis of reality, and the causes of reality - if they are removed, reality implodes and disappears. It can be seen that everything depends upon these unities for their very being, both as individuals and as the all, for without them the many could not exist; all would be one and only one.

All the Gods are ineffably united in profound superessential harmony; all are in all, and each is overflowing with goodness, wisdom, and beauty. Their number is one-infinite, and they are the superpowerful causes of all beings. The divine happiness of the Gods is concealed by the light which streams forth from their inaccessibly perfect presence; they dance with exuberant joy to their own strains and rhythms beyond the perceptions of any but Gods; even echoes of their eternal music tear at the strongest of souls, as with unresisting airs each is wafted through the immortal spheres, until with a bursting co-sensation every whole is permeated by every one, not in silence, nor yet with sound, but by the incessant purity of the Gods' own communications. Then the divine realizes the divine, and in truth they were never separate, time has receded like a dream, and what becomes a God was always a God, what becomes perfectly united ever was united in perfection, what becomes the very presence of supreme bliss always was supremely blissful, and what becomes a being of light always was a sparkling illumination from The First.

The following pieces are a treasury of magnificent ideas, and should prove to be of permanent worth and a source of inspiration to all lovers of wisdom and friends of truth.

Without the Gods how short a period stands
The proudest monument of mortal hands,

The Iliad, Trans A. Pope

Our intention in pursuing these mysteries is no other than by the logical energies of our reason to arrive at the simple intellection of beings, and by these to excite the divine one resident in the depths of our essence, or rather which presides over our essence, that we may perceive the simple and incomprehensible One. For after, through discursive energies and intellections, we have properly denied of the first principle all conditions peculiar to beings, there will be some danger, lest, deceived by imagination after numerous negations, we should think that we have arrived either at nothing, or at something slender and vain, indeterminate, formless, and confused; unless we are careful in proportion as we advance in negations to excite by a certain amatorial affection the divine vigour of our unity; trusting that by this means we may enjoy divine unity, when we have dismissed the motion of reason and the multiplicity of intelligence, and tend through unity alone to The One Itself, and through love to the supreme and ineffable Good.

Proclus

The Ascent to The Ineffable

Of all the dogmas of Plato, that concerning the first principle of things as far transcends in sublimity the doctrine of other philosophers of a different sect, on this subject, as this supreme cause of all transcends other causes. For, according to Plato, the highest God, whom in the *Republic* he calls *The Good,* and in the *Parmenides, The One,* is not only above soul and intellect, but is even superior to being itself. Hence, since every thing which can in any respect be known, or of which any thing can be asserted, must be connected with the universality of things, but the first cause is above all things, it is very properly said by Plato to be perfectly ineffable.

The first hypothesis therefore of his Parmenides,[141e-142a] in which all things are denied of this immense principle, concludes as follows:

PARM: "*The One* therefore *is* in no respect.

ARIS: So it seems.

PARM: Hence it is not in such a manner as *to be* one, for thus it would be *being,* and participate of *essence*: but as it appears, *The One* neither *is one,* nor *is,* if it be proper to believe in reasoning of this kind.

ARIS: It appears so.

PARM: But can any thing either belong to, or be affirmed of that which is not?

ARIS: How can it?

PARM: Neither therefore does any *name* belong to it, nor *discourse,* nor any *science,* nor *sense,* nor *opinion.*

ARIS: It does not appear that there can.

PARM: Hence it can neither be *named,* nor *spoken of,* nor *conceived by opinion,* nor be *known,* nor *perceived* by any being.

ARIS: So it seems."

And here it must be observed that this conclusion respecting the highest principle of things, that he is perfectly ineffable and inconceivable, is the result of a most scientific series of negations, in which not only all sensible and intellectual beings are denied of him, but even natures the most transcendently allied to him, his first and most divine progeny. For that which so eminently distinguishes the philosophy of Plato from others is this, that every part of it is stamped with the character of science.

The vulgar indeed proclaim the Deity to be ineffable; but as they have no scientific knowledge that he is so, this is nothing more than a confused and indistinct perception of the most sublime of all truths, like that of a thing seen between sleeping and waking, like Phæacia to Odysseus when sailing to his native land,

> That lay before him indistinct and vast,
> Like a broad shield amid the watr'y waste.
>
> *Odyssey. V v. 281.*

In short, an unscientific perception of the ineffable nature of the Divinity resembles that of a man, who, on surveying the heavens, should assert of the altitude of its highest part, that it surpasses that of the loftiest tree, and is therefore immeasurable. But to see this scientifically, is like a survey of this highest part of the heavens by the astronomer: for he, by knowing the height of the media between us and it, knows also scientifically that it transcends in altitude not only the loftiest tree, but the summits of air and æther, the moon, and even the sun itself.

*   *   *

Let us therefore investigate what is the ascent to the ineffable, and after what manner it is accomplished, according to Plato, from the last of things, following the profound and most inquisitive Damascius[3] as our leader in this arduous investigation. Let our discourse also be common to other principles, and to things proceeding from them to that which is last; and let us, beginning from that which is perfectly effable and known to sense, ascend to the ineffable, and establish in silence, as in a port, the parturitions of truth concerning it.

Let us then assume the following axiom, in which as in a secure vehicle we may safely pass from hence thither. I say, therefore, that the unindigent is naturally prior to the indigent. For that which is in want of another is naturally adapted from necessity to be subservient to that of which it is indigent. But if they are mutually in want of each other, each being indigent of the other in a different respect, neither of them will be the principle. For the *unindigent* is most adapted to that which is *truly the*

---

[3] This most excellent philosopher, whose MS. treatise περι αρχων is a treasury of divine science and erudition, is justly called by Simplicius ζητικωτατος, most inquisitive. See a very long and beautiful extract from this work in the Additional Notes to the *Parmenides* in the third volume of my Plato (TTS vol. XI).

principle. And if it is in want of any thing, according to this it will not be the principle. It is however necessary that the principle should be this very thing, the principle alone. The unindigent therefore pertains to this, nor must it by any means be acknowledged that there is any thing prior to it. This, however, would be acknowledged, if it had any connection with the indigent.

*   *   *

Let us then consider *body*, (that is, a triply extended substance,) endued with quality; for this is the first thing effable by us, and is sensible. Is this then the principle of things? But it is two things, body, and quality which is in body as a subject. Which of these therefore is by nature prior? For both are indigent of their proper parts: and that also which is in a subject is indigent of the subject.

Shall we say then that body itself is the principle and the first essence? But this is impossible. For, in the first place, the principle will not receive any thing from that which is posterior to itself. But body, we say, is the recipient of quality. Hence quality, and a subsistence in conjunction with it, are not derived from body, since quality is present with body as something different. And, in the second place, body is every way divisible; its several parts are indigent of each other, and the whole is indigent of all the parts. As it is indigent, therefore, and receives its completion from things which are indigent, it will not be entirely unindigent.

Further still, if it is not one but *united*, it will require, as Plato says, the connecting one. It is likewise something common and formless, being as it were a certain matter. It requires, therefore, ornament and the possession of form, that it may not be merely body, but a body with a certain particular quality; as, for instance, a fiery or earthly body, and, in short, body adorned and invested with a particular quality. Hence the things which accede to it, finish and adorn it.

Is then that which accedes the principle? But this is impossible. For it does not abide in itself, nor does it subsist alone, but is in a subject, of which also it is indigent. If, however, some one should assert that body is not a subject, but one of the elements in each, as, for instance, animal in horse and man, thus also each will be indigent of the other, *viz.* this subject, and that which is in the subject; or rather the common element, animal, and the peculiarities, as the rational and irrational, will be indigent. For elements are always indigent of each other, and that which is composed from elements is indigent of the elements.

In short, this sensible nature, and which is so manifest to us, is neither body; for this does not of itself move the senses, nor quality; for this does not possess an interval commensurate with sense. Hence, that which is the object of sight, is neither body nor colour; but coloured body, or colour corporalized, is that which is motive of the sight. And universally that which is sensible, which is body with a particular quality, is motive of sense.

From hence, it is evident that the thing which excites the sense is something incorporeal. For if it was body, it would not yet be the object of sense. Body therefore requires that which is incorporeal, and that which is incorporeal, body. For an incorporeal nature is not of itself sensible. It is, however, different from body, because these two possess prerogatives different from each other, and neither of these subsists prior to the other; but being elements of one sensible thing, they are present with each other; the one imparting interval to that which is void of interval, but the other introducing to that which is formless, sensible variety invested with form.

In the third place, neither are both these together the principle; since they are not unindigent. For they stand in need of their proper elements, and of that which conducts them to the generation of one form. For body cannot effect this, since it is of itself impotent; nor quality, since it is not able to subsist separate from the body in which it is, or together with which it has its being. The composite therefore either produces itself, which is impossible, for it does not converge to itself, but the whole of it is multifariously dispersed, or it is not produced by itself, and there is some other principle prior to it.

*   *   *

Let it then be supposed to be that which is called *nature*, being a principle of motion and rest, in that which is moved and at rest, essentially and not according to accident. For this is something more simple, and is fabricative of composite forms. If, however, it is in the things fabricated, and does not subsist separate from, nor prior to them, but stands in need of them for its being, it will not be unindigent; though it possesses something transcendent with respect to them, *viz.* the power of fashioning and fabricating them. For it has its being together with them, and has in them an inseparable subsistence; so that when they are it is, and is not when they are not, and this in consequence of perfectly verging to them, and not being able to sustain that which is appropriate. For the power of increasing, nourishing, and generating similars, and the one prior to these three, *viz.* nature, is not wholly incorporeal, but is nearly a certain quality of body, from which it alone differs, in that it imparts to the composite to be inwardly moved and at rest. For the quality of that which is sensible imparts that which is apparent in matter, and that which falls on sense.

But *body* imparts interval every way extended; and *nature*, an inwardly proceeding natural energy, whether according to place only, or according to nourishing, increasing, and generating things similar. Nature, however, is inseparable from a subject, and is indigent, so that it will not be in short the principle, since it is indigent of that which is subordinate. For it will not be wonderful, if being a certain principle, it is indigent of the principle above it; but it would be wonderful, if it were indigent of things posterior to itself, and of which it is supposed to be the principle.

$$* \quad * \quad *$$

By the like arguments we may show that the principle cannot be *irrational soul*, whether sensitive, or orectic. For if it appears that it has something separate, together with impulsive and gnostic energies, yet at the same time, it is bound in body, and has something inseparable from it; since it is not able to convert itself to itself, but its energy is mingled with its subject. For it is evident that its essence is something of this kind; since if it were liberated, and in itself free, it would also evince a certain independent energy, and would not always be converted to body; but sometimes it would be converted to itself; or though it were always converted to body, yet it would judge and explore itself.

The energies, therefore, of the multitude of mankind, though they are conversant with externals, yet at the same time they exhibit that which is separate about them. For they consult how they should engage in them, and observe that deliberation is necessary, in order to effect or be passive to apparent good, or to decline something of the contrary. But the impulses of other irrational animals are uniform and spontaneous, are moved together with the sensible organs, and require the senses alone that they may obtain from sensibles the pleasurable, and avoid the painful.

If, therefore, the body communicates in pleasure and pain, and is affected in a certain respect by them, it is evident that the psychical energies (*i.e.* energies belonging to the soul) are exerted, mingled with bodies, and are not purely psychical, but are also corporeal; for perception is of the animated body, or of the soul corporalized, though in such perception the psychical idiom predominates over the corporeal; just as in bodies the corporeal idiom has dominion according to interval and subsistence. As the irrational soul, therefore, has its being in something different from itself, so far it is indigent of the subordinate: but a thing of this kind will not be the principle.

*   *   *

Prior then to this essence, we see a certain form separate from a subject, and converted to itself, such as is the *rational nature.* Our *soul*, therefore, presides over its proper energies, and corrects itself. This, however, would not be the case, unless it was converted to itself; and it would not be converted to itself unless it had a separate essence. It is not therefore indigent of the subordinate.

Shall we then say that it is the most perfect principle? But it does not at once exert all its energies, but is always indigent of the greater part. The principle, however, wishes to have nothing indigent: but the rational nature is an essence in want of its own energies. Some one, however, may say that it is an eternal essence, and has never-failing essential energies, always concurring with its essence, according to the *self-moved*, and *ever vital*, and that it is therefore unindigent, and will be the principle. To this we reply, that the whole soul is one form and one nature, partly unindigent and partly indigent; but the principle is perfectly unindigent. Soul therefore, which exerts mutable energies, will not be the most proper principle.

*   *   *

Hence it is necessary that there should be something prior to this, which is in every respect immutable, according to nature, life, and knowledge, and according to all powers and energies, such as we assert an *eternal and immutable essence* to be, and such as is much honoured *intellect*, to which Aristotle having ascended, thought he had discovered the first principle. For what can be wanting to that which perfectly comprehends in itself its own plenitudes (πληρωματα), and of which neither addition nor ablation changes any thing belonging to it? Or is not this also, one and many, whole and parts, containing in itself, things first, middle, and last? The subordinate plenitudes also stand it need of the more excellent, and the more excellent of the subordinate, and the whole of the parts. For the things related are indigent of each other, and what are first of what are last, through the same cause; for it is not of itself that which is first.

Besides *The One* here is indigent of *the many*, because it has its subsistence in *the many*. Or it may be said, that this one is collective of the many, and this not by itself, but in conjunction with them. Hence there is much of the indigent in this principle. For since intellect generates in itself its proper plenitudes from which the whole at once receives its completion, it will be itself indigent of itself, not only that which is generated of that which generates, but also that which generates of that which is generated, in order to the whole completion of that which wholly generates itself.

Further still, intellect understands and is understood, is intellective of and intelligible to itself, and both these. Hence the intellectual is indigent of the intelligible, as of its proper object of desire; and the intelligible is in want of the intellectual, because it wishes to be the intelligible of it. Both also are indigent of either, since the possession is always accompanied with indigence, in the same manner as the world is always present with matter. Hence a certain indigence is naturally co-essentialised with intellect, so that it cannot be the most proper principle.

*   *   *

Shall we, therefore, in the next place, direct our attention to the most simple of beings, which Plato calls *the one being*, εν ον? For as there is no separation there throughout the whole, nor any multitude, or order, or duplicity, or conversion to itself, what indigence will there appear to be in the perfectly united? And especially what indigence will there be of that which is subordinate? Hence the great Parmenides ascended to this most safe principle, as that which is most unindigent.

Is it not, however, here necessary to attend to the conception of Plato, that the united is not *The One Itself*, but that which is passive[4] to it? And this being the case, it is evident that it ranks after *The One*; for it is supposed to be *the united* and not *The One Itself*.

If also *being* is composed from the elements *bound* and *infinity*, as appears from the *Philebus* of Plato, where he calls it that which is mixt, it will be indigent of its elements. Besides, if the conception of *being* is different from that of *being united*, and that which is a whole is both united and being, these will be indigent of each other, and the whole which is called *one being* is indigent of the two. And though *the one* in this is better than *being*, yet this is indigent of being, in order to the subsistence of one being. But if *being* here supervenes *the one*, as it were, form in that which is mixt and united, just as the idiom of man in that which is collectively rational-mortal-animal, thus also *the one* will be indigent of *being*.

If, however, to speak more properly, *the one* is two-fold, *this* being the cause of the mixture, and subsisting prior to being, but *that* conferring

---

[4] See the *Sophista* of Plato, where this is asserted [245a ff].

rectitude on being, - if this be the case, neither will the indigent perfectly desert this nature.

*   *   *

After all these, it may be said that *The One* will be perfectly unindigent. For neither is it indigent of that which is posterior to itself for its subsistence, since the truly one is by itself separated from all things; nor is it indigent of that which is inferior or more excellent in itself; for there is nothing in it besides itself; nor is it in want of itself. But it is one, because neither has it any duplicity with respect to itself. For not even the relation of itself to itself must be asserted of the truly one; since it is perfectly simple. This, therefore, is the most unindigent of all things. Hence this is the principle and the cause of all; and this is at once the first of all things.

If these qualities, however, are present with it, it will not be *The One*. Or may we not say that all things subsist in *The One* according to *The One*? And that both these subsist in it, and such other things as we predicate of it, as, for instance, the most simple, the most excellent, the most powerful, the preserver of all things, and the good itself? If these things, however, are thus true of *The One*, it will thus also be indigent of things posterior to itself, according to those very things which we add to it. For the principle is and is said to be the principle of things proceeding from it, and the cause is the cause of things caused, and the first is the first of things arranged posterior to it.[5]

Further still, the simple subsists according to a transcendency of other things, the most powerful according to power with relation to the subjects of it; and the good, the desirable, and the preserving, are so called with reference to things benefited, preserved, and desiring. And if it should be said, to be all things according to the preassumption of all things in itself, it will indeed be said to be so according to *The One* alone, and will at the same time be the one cause of all things prior to all, and will be this and no other according to *The One*.

So far, therefore, as it is *The One* alone, it will be unindigent; but so far as unindigent, it will be the first principle and stable root of all principles. So far, however, as it is the principle and the first cause of all things, and is preestablished as the object of desire to all things, so far it appears to be in a certain respect indigent of the things to which it is related. It has

---

[5] For a thing cannot be said to be a principle or cause without the subsistence of the things of which it is the principle or cause. Hence, so far as it is a principle or cause, it will be indigent of the subsistence of these.

therefore, if it be lawful so to speak, an ultimate vestige of indigence, just as on the contrary matter has an ultimate echo of the unindigent, or a most obscure and debile impression of *The One*.

And language indeed appears to be here subverted. For so far as it is *The One*, it is also unindigent, since the principle has appeared to subsist according to the most unindigent and *The One*. At the same time, however, so far as it is *The One*, it is also the principle; and so far as it is *The One* it is unindigent, but so far as the principle, indigent. Hence so far as it is unindigent, it is also indigent, though not according to the same; but with respect to being that which it is, it is unindigent; but as producing and comprehending other things in itself, it is indigent. This, however, is the peculiarity of *The One*; so that it is both unindigent and indigent according to *The One*. Not indeed that it is each of these, in such a manner as we divide it in speaking of it, but it is one alone; and according to this is both other things, and that which is indigent. For how is it possible it should not be indigent also so far as it is *The One*? Just as it is all other things which proceed from it. For the indigent also is something belonging to all things.

Something else, therefore, must be investigated which in no respect has any kind of indigence. But of a thing of this kind it cannot with truth be asserted that it is the principle, nor can it even be said of it that it is most unindigent, though this appears to be the most venerable of all assertions.[6] For this signifies transcendency, and an exemption from the indigent. We do not, however, think it proper to call this even *the perfectly exempt*; but that which is in every respect incapable of being apprehended, and about which we must be perfectly silent, will be the most just axiom of our conception in the present investigation; nor yet this as uttering any thing, but as rejoicing in not uttering, and by this venerating that immense unknown.

This then is the mode of ascent to that which is called the first, or rather to that which is beyond every thing which can be conceived, or become the subject of hypothesis.

From the writings of Thomas Taylor (1758 – 1835)

---

[6] See the extracts from Damascius in the additional notes to the third volume [TTS vol. XI], which contains an inestimable treasure of the most profound conceptions concerning the ineffable.

The King of All Things

All things are situated about the king of all things; and all things subsist for his sake, and he is the cause of all beautiful things. But second things are situated about that which is second; and such as are third in gradation about that which is third. The human soul therefore extends itself in order to learn the quality of these things, and looks to such particulars as are allied to itself, none of which are sufficient for the purpose. But about the king himself, and the natures of which I have spoken, there is nothing of this kind: but the soul speaks of that which is posterior to this. Indeed, O Son of Dionysius and Doris, this your inquiry concerning the cause of all beautiful things, is as of a nature endued with a certain quality. Or rather it is a parturition respecting this ingenerated in the soul; from which he who is not liberated will never in reality acquire truth. (Plato's *Second Epistle*)

Proclus' Theology of Plato, Book II

VIII Such a mode of words, therefore, neither connumerates the king of all things with the other kings, nor co-arranges him as the leader of a triad with the second and third power. For of a triadic division the first monad, indeed, is the leader of first orders, and which are co-ordinate with itself; but the second of second; and the third of third orders. If, however, some one should apprehend that the first monad is the leader of all things, so as to comprehend at once both second and third allotments; yet the cause which subsists according to comprehension is different from that which similarly pervades to all things. And to the king of all things, indeed, all things are subject according to one reason and one order; but to the first of the triad, things first are subjected according to the same order; and it is necessary that things second and third should be subservient according to their communion with the remaining kings. Does not, therefore, what is here said by Plato remarkably celebrate the exempt nature of the first cause, and his unco-ordination with the other kingdoms of the Gods? Since he says that this cause similarly reigns over all things, that all things subsist about him, and that *for his sake* essence and energy are inherent in all things.

Observe too, that Plato calls the first God king; but he does not think fit to give the others the same appellation, not only in the beginning of what he says about the first, but shortly after, he adds: "About the king himself and the natures of which I have spoken there is nothing of this kind." The first God, therefore, alone is called king. But he is called not only the king of things first, in the same manner as the second of things second, and the third of things third, but as the cause at once of all being and all beauty. Hence the first God precedes the other causes in an exempt and uniform manner, and according to a transcendency of the whole of things, and is neither celebrated by Plato as co-ordinated with them, nor as the leader of a triad.

But when Plato a little after says, "This your inquiry concerning the cause of all beautiful things is as of a nature endued with *a certain quality*," he clearly indicates that neither language nor knowledge is adapted to that which is first: for, as being unknown, it cannnot be apprehended by intelligence, and as being uncircumscribed, it cannot be explained by words. But whatever you may say of it, you will speak as of a *certain thing;* and you will speak indeed *about* it, but you will not speak *it*. For speaking of the things of which it is the cause, we are unable to say, or to apprehend through intelligence what it is.

Here therefore, the addition of quality, and the busy energy of the soul, remove it from the goodness which is exempt from all things, by the redundancy of its conceptions about it. This likewise draws the soul down to kindred, connate, and multiform intelligibles, and prevents her from receiving that which is characterized by unity, and is occult in the participation of *The Good*. And it is not only proper that the human soul should be purified from things co-ordinate with itself in the union and communion with that which is first, and that for this purpose it should leave all the multitude of itself behind, and exciting its own hyparxis, approach with closed eyes, as it is said, to the king of all things, and participate of his light, as much as this is lawful for it to accomplish; but intellect also, which is prior to us, and all divine natures, by their highest unions, superessential torches, and first hyparxes are united to that which is first, and always participate of its exuberant fullness; and this not so far as they are that which they are, but so far as they are exempt from things allied to themselves, and converge to the one principle of all. For the cause of all disseminated in all things impressions of his own all-perfect transcendency, and through these establishes all things about himself, and being exempt from the whole of things, *is ineffably present to all things. Every thing therefore, entering into the ineffable of its own nature, finds there the symbol of the father of all.* All things too naturally venerate him, and are united to him, through an appropriate mystic impression, divesting themselves of their own nature, and hastening to become his impression alone, and to participate him alone, through the desire of his unknown nature, and of the fountain of good. Hence, when they have run upwards as far as to this cause, they become tranquil, and are liberated from the parturitions and the desire which all things naturally possess of goodness unknown, ineffable, imparticipable, and transcendentally full. But that what is here said is concerning the first God, and that Plato in these conceptions leaves him unco-ordinated with and exempt from the other causes, has been, I think, sufficiently evinced.

IX Let us in the next place consider each of the dogmas, and adapt them to our conceptions concerning cause, that from these we may comprehend by a reasoning process, the scope of the whole of Plato's theology.

Let then one truth concerning the first principle be especially that which celebrates his *ineffable, simple,* and *all-transcending nature*; which establishes all things about him, but does not assert that he generates or produces any thing, or that he pre-subsists as the end of things posterior to himself. For such a form of words neither adds any thing to the unknown, who is exempt from all things, nor multiplies him who is established above all union, nor refers the habitude and communion of things secondary to him who is perfectly imparticipable. Nor in short, does it announce that it teaches any thing about him, or concerning his nature, but about the second and third natures which subsist after him.

Such then being this indication of the first God, and such the manner in which it venerates the ineffable, the second to this is that which converts all the desires of things to him, and celebrates him as the object of desire to and common end of all things, according to one cause which precedes all other causes. For the last of things subsists only for the sake of something else, but the first is that only for the sake of which *all* other things subsist: and all the intermediate natures participate of these two peculiarities. Hence they genuinely adhere to the natures which surpass them, as objects of desire, but impart the perfection of desires to subordinate beings.

The third speculation of the principle of things is far inferior to the preceding, considering him as giving subsistence to all beautiful things. For to celebrate him as the supplier of good, and as end preceding the two orders of things, is not very remote from the narration which says, that all causes are posterior to him, and derive their subsistence from him, as well those which are paternal, and the sources of good, as those that are the suppliers of prolific powers. But to ascribe to him a producing and generative cause, is still more remote from the all-perfect union of the first. For as it cannot be known or discussed by language, by secondary natures, it must not be said that it is the cause, or that it is generative of beings, but we should celebrate in silence this ineffable nature, and this perfectly causeless cause which is prior to all causes. If, however, as we endeavour to ascribe to him *The Good* and *The One*, we in like manner attribute to him *cause*, and that which is *final* or *paternal*, we must pardon the parturition of the soul about this ineffable principle, aspiring to perceive him with the eye of intellect, and to speak about him; but, at the same time, the exempt transcendency of *The One* which is immense, must be considered as surpassing an indication of this kind.

From these things therefore, we may receive the sacred conceptions of Plato, and an order adapted to things themselves. And we may say that the first part of this sentence sufficiently indicates the simplicity, transcendency, and in short the unco-ordination with all things of the king of all. For the assertion that all things subsist about him, unfolds the hyparxis of things second, but leaves that which is beyond all things without any connexion with things posterior to it. But the second part celebrates the cause of all the Gods as prearranged in the order of *end*. For that which is the highest of all causes, is immediately conjoined with that which is prior to cause; but of this kind is the final cause, and that for the sake of which all things subsist. This part therefore is posterior to the other, and is woven together with the order of things, and the progression of the Platonic doctrine.

Again, the third part asserts him to be productive of all beautiful things, and thus adds to him a species of cause inferior to the final. Whence also Plotinus, I think, does not hesitate to call the first God the fountain of the beautiful. It is necessary therefore to attribute that which is best to the best of all things, that he may be the cause of all, and in reality prior to cause. But this is *The Good*.

This too, which is an admirable circumstance, may be seen in the words of Plato, that the first of these three divine dogmas, neither presumes to say any thing about *The Good*,, and this ineffable nature, nor does it permit us to refer any species of cause to it. But the second dogma leaves indeed *The Good* ineffable, as it is fit it should, but from the habitude of things posterior to it, enables us to collect the final cause; for it does not refuse to call it that for the sake of which all things subsist. But when it asserts that all things are for the sake of *The Good*, it excites in us the conception of the communion and co-ordination of that which is the object of desire with the desiring natures. And the third dogma evinces that *The Good* is the cause of all beautiful things. But this is to say something concerning it, and to add to the simplicity of the first cause, and not to abide in the conceptions of the end, but to conjoin with it the producing principle of things second. And it appears to me that Plato here indicates the natures which are proximately unfolded into light after the first. For it is not possible to say any thing concerning it except at one time being impelled to this from all things, and at another from the best of things: for it is the cause of hyparxis to all things, and unfolds its own separate union through the peculiarities of these.

We ascribe to it therefore *The One* and *The Good,* from the donation which pervades to all things from it. For of those things of which all participate, we say there is no other cause than that which is established prior to all these. But *the about* which, *the on account of which,* and *the from which,* particularly subsist in the intelligible Gods: and from these they are ascribed to the first God. For whence can we suppose the unical Gods derive their peculiarities, except from that which is prior to them? To this summit of intelligibles therefore the term *about* is adapted, because all the divine orders occultly proceed about this summit which is arranged prior to them. But the term *on account of which* pertains to the middle order of intelligibles: for all things subsist for the sake of eternity and an hyparxis perfectly entire. And the term *from which* is adapted to the extremity of intelligibles: for this first produces all things, and adorns them uniformly.

From

A Common Hymn, Proclus:

Hail! may the blissful road of life be mine,
With ev'ry good replete of light divine:
And from my members dire disease expel,
That splendid-gifted health with me may dwell.
My soul insanely wand'ring on the earth,
Though intellectual regions gave her birth,
Attract to heav'n with vigour unconfin'd,
Through mysteries which rouse the dormant mind.
Your helping hands, all-bounteous powers, extend,
And paths divine unfold as I ascend.
Give me to see those beams of glorious light,
Which aid the soul from Generation's night,
Dark, dreary, dire, indignantly to fly,
And rapidly regain her native sky.
Extend your hands, and with your fav'ring gales,
While bound for home I raise th'impatient sails,
Impel my vessel o'er life's stormy main,
Till the fair port of Piety I gain;
For there my soul, with mighty toils oppress'd,
Shall find her long-lost Paradise of rest.

The Platonic Philosophers' Creed.

The following summary of Platonic philosophy was written by Taylor and published several times with minor variations: this particular version is from Thomas M Johnson's magazine, The Platonist. It is called the 'Platonic Philsophers' Creed' with the expectation that students of philosophy will use it not so much as a dogmatic statement that admits of no argument, but rather as a starting point for a series of studies and meditations.

1 I believe that there is one first cause of all things, whose nature is so immensely transcendent, that it is even superessential; and that in consequence of this it cannot properly either be named or spoken of, or conceived by opinion, or be known, or perceived by any being.

2 I believe, however, that if it be lawful to give a name to that which is truly ineffable, the appellations of *The One* and *The Good* are of all others the most adapted to it; the former of these names indicating that it is the principle of all things, and the latter that it is the ultimate object of desire to all things.

3 I believe that this immense principle produced such things as are first and proximate to itself, most similar to itself; just as the heat *immediately* proceeding from fire is most similar to the heat in the fire; and the light *immediately* emanating from the sun, to that which the sun essentially contains. Hence, this principle produces many principles proximately from itself.

4 I likewise believe that since all things differ from each other, and are multiplied with their proper differences, each of these multitudes is suspended from its one proper principle. That, in consequence of this, all beautiful things, whether in souls or in bodies, are suspended from one fountain of beauty. That whatever possesses symmetry, and whatever is true, and all principles are in a certain respect connate with the first principle, so far as they are principles, with an appropriate subjection and analogy. That all other principles are comprehended in this first principle, not with interval and multitude, but as parts in the whole, and number in the monad. That it is not a certain principle like each of the rest; for of these, one is the principle of beauty, another of truth, and another of something else, but it is *simply principle*. Nor is it simply the *principle of beings* but it is *the principle of principles*: it being necessary that the characteristic property of principle after the same

manner as other things, should not begin from multitude, but should be collected into one monad as a summit, and which is the principle of principles.

5 I believe, therefore, that such things as are produced by the first good in consequence of being connascent with it, do not recede from essential goodness, since they are immovable and unchanged, and are eternally established in the same blessedness. All other natures, however, being produced by the one good, and many goodnesses, since they fall off from essential goodness, and are not immovably established in the nature of divine goodness, possess on this account the good according to participation.

6 I believe that as all things considered as subsisting *causally* in this immense principle, are transcendently more excellent than they are when considered as effects proceeding from him; this principle is very properly said to be all things, *prior* to all; *priority* denoting exempt transcendency. Just as number may be considered as subsisting occultly in the monad, and the circle in the centre; this *occult* being the same in each with *causal* subsistence.

7 I believe that the most proper mode of venerating this great principle of principles is to extend in silence the ineffable parturitions of the soul to its ineffable co-sensation; and that if it be at all lawful to celebrate it, it is to be celebrated as a thrice unknown darkness, as the God of all Gods, and the unity of all unities, as more ineffable than all silence, and more occult than all essence, as holy among the holies, and concealed in its first progeny, the intelligible Gods.

8 I believe that self-subsistent natures are the immediate offspring of this principle, if it be lawful thus to denominate things which ought rather to be called ineffable unfoldings into light from the ineffable.

9 I believe that incorporeal forms or ideas resident in a divine intellect, are the paradigms or models of every thing which has a perpetual subsistence according to nature. That these ideas subsist primarily in the highest intellects, secondarily in souls, and ultimately in sensible natures; and that they subsist in each, characterised by the essential properties of the beings in which they are contained. That they possess a *paternal, producing, guardian, connecting, perfective* and *uniting* power. That in *divine beings* they possess a power fabricative and gnostic; in *nature* a power fabricative but not gnostic: and in *human souls* in their present condition through a degradation of intellect, a power gnostic, but not fabricative.

10 I believe that this world, depending on its divine artificer, who is himself an intelligible world, replete with the archetypal ideas of all things, is perpetually flowing, and perpetually advancing to being, and, compared with its paradigm, has no stability, or reality of being. That considered, however, as animated by a divine soul, and as being the receptacle of divinities from whom bodies are suspended, it is justly called by Plato, a blessed God.

11 I believe that the great body of this world, which subsists in a perpetual dispersion of temporal extension, may be properly called a *whole, with a total subsistence,* or a *whole of wholes,* on account of the perpetuity of its duration, though this is nothing more than a flowing eternity. That the other wholes which it contains are the celestial spheres, the sphere of æther, the whole of air considered as one great orb, the whole earth, and the whole sea. That these spheres are *parts with a total subsistence,* and through this subsistence are perpetual.

12 I believe that all the parts of the universe, are unable to participate of the providence of divinity in a similar manner, but some of its parts enjoy this eternally, and others temporally; some in a primary and others in a secondary degree; for the universe being a perfect whole, must have a first, a middle, and a last part. But its first parts, as having the most excellent subsistence, must always exist according to nature; and its last parts must sometimes exist according to, and sometimes contrary to nature. Hence the celestial bodies, which are the first parts of the universe, perpetually subsist according to nature, both the whole spheres, and the multitude co-ordinate to these wholes; and the only alteration which they experience is a mutation of figure, and variation of light at different periods; but in the sublunary region, while the spheres of the elements remain on account of their subsistence, as wholes, always according to nature; the parts of the wholes have sometimes a natural, and sometimes an unnatural subsistence: for thus alone can the circle of generation unfold all the variety which it contains. The different periods therefore in which these mutations happen, are with great propriety called by Plato, periods of *fertility* and *sterility*: for in these periods a fertility or sterility of men, animals, and plants, takes place; so that in fertile periods mankind will be both more numerous, and upon the whole superior in mental and bodily endowments to the men of a barren period. And a similar reasoning must be extended to irrational animals and plants. The most dreadful consequence, likewise, attending a barren period with respect to mankind is this, that in such a period they have no

scientific theology, and deny the existence of the immediate progeny of the ineffable cause of all things.

13 I believe that as the divinities are eternally good and profitable, but are never noxious, and ever subsist in the same uniform mode of being, we are conjoined with them through similitude when we are virtuous, but separated from them through dissimilitude when we are vicious. That while we live according to virtue we partake of the Gods, but cause them to be our enemies when we become evil: not that they are angry (for anger is a passion, and they are impassive,) but because guilt prevents us from receiving the illuminations of the Gods, and subjects us to the power of dæmons of fateful justice. Hence, I believe, that if we obtain pardon of our guilt through prayers and sacrifices, we neither appease the Gods, nor cause any mutation to take place in them; but by methods of this kind, and by our conversion to a divine nature, we apply a remedy to our vices, and again become partakers of the goodness of the Gods. So that it is the same thing to assert, that divinity is turned from the evil, as to say that the sun is concealed from those who are deprived of sight.

14 I believe that a divine nature is not indigent of any thing. But the honours which are paid to the Gods are performed for the sake of the advantage of those who pay them. Hence, since the providence of the Gods is extended every where, a certain habitude or fitness is all that is requisite for the reception of their beneficent communications. But all habitude is produced through imitation and similitude. On this account temples imitate the heavens, but altars the earth. Statues resemble life, and on this account they are similar to animals. Herbs and stones resemble matter; and animals which are sacrificed, the irrational life of our souls. From all these, however, nothing happens to the Gods beyond what they already possess; for what accession can be made to a divine nature? But a conjunction of our souls with the Gods is by these means effected.

15 I believe that as the world considered as one great comprehending whole is a divine animal, so likewise every whole which it contains is a world, possessing in the first place a self-perfect unity proceeding from the ineffable, by which it becomes a God; in the second place, a divine intellect; in the third place, a divine soul; and in the last place a deified body. That each of these wholes is the producing cause of all the multitude which it contains, and on this account is said to be a whole prior to parts; because considered as possessing an eternal form which holds all its parts together, and gives to the whole perpetuity of subsistence, it is not indigent of such parts to the perfection of its being.

And it follows by a geometrical necessity, that these wholes which rank thus high in the universe must be animated.

16 Hence I believe that after the immense principle of principles in which all things causally subsist absorbed in superessential light, and involved in unfathomable depths, a beautiful series of principles proceeds, all largely partaking of the ineffable, all stamped with the occult characters of deity, all possessing an overflowing fullness of good. From these dazzling summits, these ineffable blossoms, these divine propagations - being, life, intellect, soul, nature and body depend; *monads* suspended from *unities*, deified natures proceeding from deities. That each of these monads is the leader of a series which extends to the last of things, and which, while it proceeds from, at the same time abides in, and returns to its leader Thus all beings proceed from, and are comprehended in the first being; all intellects emanate from one first intellect; all souls from one first soul; all natures blossom from one first nature; and all bodies proceed from the vital and luminous body of the world. That all these great monads are comprehended in the first one, from which both they and all their depending series are unfolded into light. And hence this first one is truly the unity of unities, the monad of monads, the principle of principles, the God of gods, one and all things, and yet one prior to all.

17 I also believe, that of the Gods some are mundane, but others super-mundane; and that the mundane are those who fabricate the world. But of the supermundane, some produce essences, others intellect, and others soul; and on this account, they are distinguished into three orders. Of the mundane Gods also, some are the causes of the existence of the world; others animate it; others again harmonise it, thus composed of different natures; and lastly, others guard and preserve it when harmonically arranged. Since these orders are four, and each consists of things first, middle, and last, it is necessary that the governors of these should be twelve. Hence Zeus, Poseidon, and Hephaestus, fabricate the world; Demeter, Hera, and Artemis, animate it; Hermes, Aphrodite, and Apollo, harmonise it; and lastly, Hestia, Athena, and Ares, preside over it with a guardian power. But the truth of this, may be seen in statues, as in enigmas. For Apollo harmonises the lyre; Pallas Athena is invested with arms; and Aphrodite is naked; since harmony produces beauty, and beauty is not concealed in subjects of sensible inspection. I likewise believe that as these Gods primarily possess the world, it is necessary to consider the other mundane Gods as subsisting in them; as Dionysius in Zeus, Aesculapius in Apollo, and the Graces in Aphrodite. We may also

behold the spheres with which they are connected, *viz*. Hestia with the earth, Poseidon with water, Hera with air, and Hephaestus with fire. But Apollo and Artemis are assumed for the sun and moon; the sphere of Kronos is attributed to Demeter; Æther to Pallas; and heaven is common to them all.

18 I also believe that man is a microcosm, comprehending in himself *partially* every thing which the world contains divinely and *totally*. That hence he is endued with an intellect subsisting in energy, and a rational soul proceeding from the same causes as those from which the intellect and soul of the universe proceed. And that he has likewise an ethereal vehicle analogous to the heavens, and a terrestrial body composed from the four elements, and with which also it is co-ordinate.

19 I believe that the rational part of man, in which his essence consists, is of a self-motive nature, and that it subsists between intellect, which is immovable both in essence and energy, and nature, which both moves and is moved.

20 I believe that the human as well as every mundane soul, uses periods and restitutions of its proper life. For in consequence of being measured by time, it energizes transitively, and possesses a proper motion. But every thing which is moved perpetually, and participates of time, revolves periodically, and proceeds from the same to the same.

21 I also believe that as the human soul ranks among the number of those souls that *sometimes* follow the mundane divinities, in consequence of subsisting immediately after angels, dæmons and heroes the *perpetual* attendants of the Gods, it possesses a power of descending infinitely into the sublunary region, and of ascending from thence to real being. That in consequence of this, the soul, while an inhabitant of earth, is in a fallen condition, an apostate from deity, an exile from the orb of light. That she can only be restored, while on earth, to the divine likeness, and be able after death to re-ascend to the intelligible world, by the exercise of the *cathartic*, and *theoretic* virtues; the former purifying her from the defilements of a mortal nature, and the latter elevating her to the vision of true being. And that such a soul returns after death to her kindred star from which she fell, and enjoys a blessed life.

22 I believe that the human soul essentially contains all knowledge, and that whatever knowledge she acquires in the present life, is nothing more than a recovery of what she once possessed; and which discipline evocates from its dormant retreats.

23 I also believe that the soul is punished in a future for the crimes she has committed in the present life; but that this punishment is proportioned to the crimes, and is not perpetual; divinity punishing, not from anger or revenge, but in order to purify the guilty soul, and restore her to the proper perfection of her nature.

24 I also believe that the human soul on its departure from the present life, will, if not properly purified, pass into other terrene bodies; and that if it passes into a human body, it becomes the soul of that body; but if into the body of a brute, it does not become the soul of the brute, but is externally connected with the brutal soul in the same manner as presiding dæmons are connected, in their beneficent operations, with mankind; for the rational part never becomes the soul of the irrational nature.

25 Lastly, I believe that souls that live according to virtue, shall in other respects be happy; and when separated from the irrational nature, and purified from all body, shall be conjoined with the Gods, and govern the whole world, together with the deities by whom it was produced.

The end of the Platonic (philosophic) teaching is:

"That the learner who possesses science may be sufficiently able to distinguish the genera of beings, *and to survey in perfection the definite causes of things*; where they originate; how many are their orders; how they subsist in every order of things; how they are participated; how they causally comprehend all things in themselves."

Proclus, Comm. Parmenides

The Platonic Panorama

Collected from the writings of Plato, Proclus and Thomas Taylor.

The scientific reasoning from which this dogma is deduced is the following: As the principle of all things is *The One,* it is necessary that the progression of beings should be continued, and that no vacuum should intervene either in incorporeal or corporeal natures. It is also necessary that every thing which has a natural progression should proceed through similitude. In consequence of this, it is likewise necessary that every producing principle should generate a number of the same order with itself, *viz. nature,* a natural number; *soul,* one that is psychical (*i.e.* belonging to soul); and *intellect,* an intellectual number. For if whatever possesses a power of generating, generates similars prior to dissimilars, every cause must deliver its own form and characteristic peculiarity to its progeny; and before it generates that which gives subsistence to progressions far distant and separate from its nature, it must constitute things proximate to itself according to essence, and conjoined with it through similitude. It is therefore necessary from these premises, since there is one unity the principle of the universe, that this unity should produce from itself, prior to every thing else, a multitude of natures characterised by unity, and a number the most of all things allied to its cause; and these natures are no other than the Gods.

According to this theology therefore, from the immense principle of principles, in which all things causally subsist, absorbed in superessential light, and involved in unfathomable depths, a beauteous progeny of principles proceed, all largely partaking of the ineffable, all stamped with the occult characters of deity, all possessing an overflowing fullness of good. From these dazzling summits, these ineffable blossoms, these divine propagations, being, life, intellect, soul, nature and body depend; *monads* suspended from *unities,* deified natures proceeding from deities. Each of these monads too, is the leader of a series which extends from itself to the last of things, and which while it proceeds from, at the same time abides in, and returns to its leader. And all these principles and all their progeny are finally centred and rooted by their summits in the first great all-comprehending one. Thus all beings proceed from, and are comprehended in the first being; all intellects emanate from one first intellect; all souls from one first soul; all natures blossom from one first nature; and all bodies proceed from the vital and luminous body of the world. And lastly, all these great monads are comprehended in the first one, from which both they and all their depending series are unfolded into light. Hence this first one is truly the unity of unities, the monad of monads, the principle of principles, the God of Gods, one and all things, and yet one prior to all.

No objections of any weight, no arguments but such as are sophistical, can be urged against this most sublime theory which is so congenial to the unperverted conceptions of the human mind, that it can only be treated with ridicule and contempt in degraded, barren, and barbarous ages.

That which is the first of all things therefore, unfolds into light all the Gods, divine souls, and the more excellent genera, and is neither complicated with its progeny, nor multiplied about them; but being perfectly exempt from them in an admirable simplicity, and transcendency of union, it imparts to all things indifferently progression and at the same time order in the progression.

Thus, all the processions of the Gods after the One, may be comprehended in six orders:

> The Intelligible Gods,
> The Intelligible and at the same time Intellectual Gods,
> The Intellectual Gods,
> The Supermundane Gods,
> The Liberated Gods,
> The Mundane Gods,

whose spheres or worlds are characterised by the Monads suspended from Them, that is,

> Being,
> Life,
> Intellect,
> Soul,
> Nature,
> Body,

respectively. All these Monads are in each Order of the Gods, in a manner corresponding to their several peculiarities; hence they subsist essentially in Being, vivifically or vitally in Life, intellectually in Intellect, psychically in Soul, formatively in Nature, and materially in Body. And further, in Intelligibles, Being is according to *essence*, but Life and Intellect are according to *cause*; in Intelligible-Intellectuals, Intellect is according to *cause*, Being according to *participation*, and Life according to *essence*; and in

Intellectuals, Intellect is according to *essence*, but Being and Life are according to *participation*.

Thus, the *intelligible order* holds the first rank, and must consist of *being, life,* and *intellect; i.e.* must *abide, proceed,* and *return,* and this superessentially; at the same time that it is characterised, or subsists principally according to *permanent being.* But in the next place that which is both *intelligible* and *intellectual* succeeds, which must likewise be triple, but must principally subsist according to *life* or *intelligence.* And in the third place the *intellectual* order must succeed, which is *triply convertive,* and principally subsists according to intellect.

But as in consequence of the existence of the sensible world, it is necessary that there should be some demiurgic cause of its existence, this cause can only be found in *intellect,* and in the last hypostasis of the *intellectual triad.* For all forms in this hypostasis subsist according to all-various and perfect divisions; and forms can only fabricate when they have a perfect intellectual separation from each other. But since *fabrication* is nothing more than *procession,* the demiurgus will be to the posterior orders of Gods what *The One* is to the orders prior to the *demiurgus;* and consequently he will be that secondarily which the first cause of all is primarily. Hence his first production will be an order of Gods analogous to the *intelligible order,* and which is denominated *super-mundane.* After this he must produce an order of Gods similar to the *intelligible* and *intellectual* order, and which are denominated *liberated* Gods. And in the last place, a procession correspondent to the *intellectual order,* and which can be no other than the mundane Gods. For the demiurgus is chiefly characterised according to diversity, and is allotted the boundary of all universal hypostases.

Every order of gods commences from a *monad,* or proximately exempt producing cause: for it is necessary, that every divine cause should be to its progeny what the first cause is to all the divine orders: since it can no otherwise produce in the best manner, than by imitating that which is best. But the first cause in an *imparticipable* one, or, in other words, is not consubsistent with his progeny; and hence every divine order must have a presubsisting and primary principle of its progression, which, from its similitude to the first cause, is very properly called a *monad.* The immediate progeny, too, of every divine monad, must be exquisitely allied to the monad its cause, since the similar, in every well-ordered progression, must always subsist prior to the dissimilar.

This being premised, the reader, who *knows scientifically* the number of the divine orders, may easily collect, that *as the ineffable one,* who is superior to an intelligible essence, is the *monad* of first intelligibles, which he illuminates with superessential light: so *Phanes*, or *intelligible intellect*, which is the extremity of the intelligible order, is the *monad* of *intellectuals*, whom he illuminates with intelligible light. In like manner *Jupiter*, who is the boundary of the gods, *properly called intellectual*, is the *king* or *monad* of the *supermundane gods*, whom he illuminates with intellectual light; and consequently the *Sun* must subsist at the extremity of the supermundane order, must be the *monad* of the *mundane gods*, and must illuminate sensible natures with *supermundane light*: for otherwise the mundane gods would not be suspended from a monad analogous to the other divine orders. And lastly, *Bacchus*, or the *mundane intellect*, is the *monad* of the *Titans*, or the *ultimate artificers of things*, whom he illuminates with *light of a mundane* characteristic. Hence, Bacchus is the cause of the mundane properties of light, *viz.* of those properties which are inseparable from a corporeal nature, and which are found to subsist in visible light: for light, as I have elsewhere shewn from Proclus, is an immaterial body.

Self-subsistent superessential natures therefore are the immediate progeny of *The One*, if it be lawful thus to denominate things, which ought rather to be called ineffable unfoldings into light from the ineffable; for progeny implies a producing cause, and *The One* must be conceived as something more excellent than this. From this divine self-perfect and self-producing multitude, a series of self-perfect natures, *viz.* of beings, lives, intellects, and souls proceeds, according to Plato, in the last link of which luminous series he also classes the human soul; proximately suspended from the dæmoniacal order:[7] for this order, as he clearly asserts in the *Banquet*, "stands in the middle rank between the divine and human, fills up the vacant space, and links together all intelligent nature."

The reader who *profoundly* understands this theory, may consider himself as possessing the key which easily opens the treasury of the highest Wisdom: but let not any one who has not *legitimately* studied the philosophy of Plato, deceive himself by supposing that this theory may be understood by barely reading over the above observations; for it is certainly ridiculous in the extreme to imagine that a theory like the preceding, which respects the most sublime objects of speculation, which is the result of the most consummate science, and which depends on a variety of previous disciplines, can be apprehended as soon as mentioned: the man that can entertain an opinion so stupid and arrogant,

---

[7] That order which includes angels, daemons and heroes.

is not only *ignorant* in matters of the highest importance, but is even *ignorant of his ignorance.*

That after the great incomprehensible cause of all, a divine multitude subsists, co-operating with this cause in the production and government of the universe, has always been and is still admitted by all nations, and all religions, however much they may differ in their opinions respecting the nature of the subordinate deities, and the veneration which is to be paid to them by man; and however barbarous the conceptions of some nations on this subject may be when compared with those of others. Hence, says the elegant Maximus Tyrius, "You will see one according law and assertion in all the earth, that there is one God, the king and father of all things, and many Gods, sons of God, ruling together with him. This the Greek says, and the Barbarian says, the inhabitant of the Continent, and he who dwells near the sea, the wise and the unwise. And if you proceed as far as to the utmost shores of the ocean, there also there are Gods, rising very near to some, and setting very near to others."

And this is the best employment of our energy: to be extended to a divine nature itself, having our powers at rest, to revolve harmoniously round it, to excite all the multitude of the soul to this union, and laying aside all such things as are posterior to *The One*, to become seated and conjoined with that which is ineffable, and beyond all things. For the soul when looking at things posterior to herself, beholds the shadows and images of beings, but when she converts herself to herself she evolves her own essence, and the reasons which she contains. And at first indeed, she only as it were beholds herself; but, when she penetrates more profoundly into the knowledge of herself, she finds in herself both intellect, and the orders of beings. When however, she proceeds into her interior recesses, and into the adytum as it were of the soul, she perceives with her eye closed, the genus of the Gods, and the unities of beings. For *all* things are in us psychically, and through this we are naturally capable of knowing all things, by exciting the powers and the images of wholes which we contain.

Whether therefore, it be lawful to denominate *The One* the fountain of deity, or the kingdom of beings, or the unity of all unities, or the goodness which is generative of truth, or an hyparxis exempt from all these things, and beyond all causes, both the paternal and the generative, let it be honoured by us in silence, and prior to silence by union, and of the mystic end may it impart by illumination a portion adapted to our souls.

The Gods

Plotinus, Ennead V, viii.

All the Gods are venerable and beautiful, and their beauty is immense. What else however is it but intellect through which they are such? and because intellect energizes in them in so great a degree as to render them visible [by its light]? For it is not because their bodies are beautiful. For those Gods that have bodies, do not through this derive their subsistence as Gods; but these also are Gods through intellect. For they are not at one time wise, and at another destitute of wisdom; but they are always wise, in an impassive, stable, and pure intellect. They likewise know all things, not human concerns [precedaneously] but their own, which are divine, and such as intellect sees.

Of the Gods however, those that are in the sensible heaven, for they abound in leisure, always contemplate, as if remotely, what the intelligible heaven contains, and this with an elevated head. But those that dwell in the latter, occupy the whole of the heaven, which is there, and survey [its blessed] inhabitants. For all things there are heaven, and there the earth is heaven, as also are the sea, animals, plants, and men. And in short, every thing pertaining to that heaven is celestial.

The Gods likewise that it contains do not think men undeserving of their regard, nor any thing else that is there [because every thing there is divine]. And they occupy and pervade without ceasing the whole of that [blissful] region. For the life which is there is unattended with labour, and truth [as Plato says in the *Phædrus*] is their generator, and nutriment, their essence and nurse. They likewise see all things, not those with which generation, but those with which essence is present. And they perceive themselves in others. For all things there are diaphanous; and nothing is dark and resisting, but every thing is apparent to every one internally and throughout. For light every where meets with light: since every thing contains all things in itself, and again sees all things in another. So that all things are every where, and all is all. Each thing likewise is every thing. And the splendour there is infinite. For every thing there is great, since even that which is small is great.

The sun too which is there is all the stars: and again each star is the sun and all the stars. In each, however, a different property predominates, but at the same time all things are visible in each. Motion likewise there is pure; for the motion is not confounded by a mover different from it. Permanency also suffers no change of its nature, because it is not mingled with the unstable. And the beautiful there is beautiful, because it does not subsist in beauty [as in a subject].

Each thing too is there established, not as in a foreign land, but the seat of each thing is that which each thing is; and concurs with it, while it proceeds as it were on high from whence it originated. Nor is the thing itself different from the place in which it subsists. For the subject of it is intellect, and it is itself intellect. Just as if some one should conceive that stars germinate from the light of this visible heaven which is luminous. In this sensible region therefore, one part is not produced from another, but each part is alone a part. But there each part always proceeds from the whole, and is at the same time each part and the whole. For it appears indeed as a part; but by him whose sight is acute, it will be seen as a whole; *viz*. by him whose sight resembles that which Lynceus is said to have possessed, and which penetrated the interior parts of the earth; the fable obscurely indicating the acuteness of the vision of supernal eyes.

There is likewise no weariness of the vision which is there, nor any plenitude of perception which can bring intuition to an end. For neither was there any vacuity, which when filled might cause the visive energy to cease: nor is this one thing, but that another, so as to occasion a part of one thing not to be amicable with that of another. Whatever likewise is there, possesses an untamed and unwearied power. And that which is there insatiable is so, because its plenitude never causes it to despise that by which it is filled. For by seeing it more abundantly sees, and perceiving both itself and the objects of its perception to be infinite, it follows its own nature [in unceasing contemplation]. And life indeed is not wearisome to any one, when it is pure. Why, therefore, should that which leads the most excellent life be weary?

But the life there is wisdom; a wisdom not obtained by a reasoning process, because the whole of it always was, and is not in any respect deficient, so as to be in want of investigation. But it is the first wisdom, and is not derived from another.

From the Parmenides of Plato

Parmenides: Neither, therefore, is time present with The One, nor does it subsist in any time.

Socrates: It does not, indeed, according to the decisions of reason.

Parmenides: What then? Do not the terms *it was*, *it has been*, *it did become*, seem to signify the participation of the time past?

Socrates: Certainly.

Parmenides: And do not the terms *it will be*, *it may become*, and *it will be generated*, signify that which is about to be hereafter?

Socrates: Certainly.

Parmenides: But are not the terms *it is*, and *it is becoming to be*, marks of the present time?

Socrates: Entirely so.

Parmenides: If then *The One* participates in no respect of any time, it neither ever *was*, nor *has been*, nor *did become*: nor is it *now generated*, nor is *becoming to be*, nor *is*, nor *may become* hereafter, nor *will be generated*, nor *will be*.

Socrates: It is most true.

Parmenides: Is it possible, therefore, that any thing can participate of essence, except according to some one of these?

Socrates: It is not.

Parmenides: In no respect, therefore, does *The One* participate of essence.

Socrates: It does not appear that it can.

Parmenides: *The One*, therefore, *is* in no respect.

Socrates: So it seems.

Parmenides: Hence, it is not in such a manner as *to be* one, for thus it would be being, and participate of essence: but, as it appears, the one neither *is one* nor *is*, if it be proper to believe in reasoning of this kind.

Socrates: It appears so.

Parmenides: But can any thing either belong to, or be affirmed of, that which is not?

Socrates: How can it?

Parmenides: Neither, therefore, does any name belong to it, nor discourse, nor any science, nor sense, nor opinion.

Socrates: It does not appear that there can.

Parmenides: Hence, it can neither be named, nor spoken of, nor conceived by opinion, nor be known, nor perceived by any being.

Socrates: So it seems.

Parmenides: Is it possible, therefore, that these things can thus take place about *The One*?

Socrates: It does not appear to me that they can.   (141d-e)

The Providence of the Gods

Proclus, Theology of Plato, I, 17

The very being of the Gods is defined by the good, and in this they have their subsistence.

But to provide for things of a subject nature, is to confer on them a certain good.

How, therefore, can we deprive the Gods of providence, without at the same time depriving them of goodness?

And how if we subvert their goodness is it possible, that we should not also ignorantly subvert their hyparxis?

Hence it is necessary to admit as a thing consequent to the very being of the Gods that they are good according to every virtue. And again, it is consequent to this that they do not withdraw themselves from a providential attention to secondary natures, either through indolence, or imbecility, or ignorance. But to this I think it is also consequent that there is with them the most excellent knowledge, unpolluted power, and unenvying and exuberant will. From which it appears that they provide for the whole of things, and omit nothing which is requisite to the supply of good.

Let no one think that the Gods extend such a providence about secondary things, as is either of a busy or laborious nature, or that this is the case with their exempt transcendency, which is established remote from mortal difficulty. For their blessedness is not willing to be defiled with the difficulty of administration, since even the life of good men is accompanied with facility, and is void of molestation and pain. But all labours and molestation arise from the impediments of matter.

If, however, it be requisite to define the mode of the providence of the Gods, it must be admitted that it is spontaneous, unpolluted, immaterial, and ineffable. For the Gods do not govern all things either by investigating what is fit, or exploring the good of every thing by ambiguous reasonings, or by looking externally, and following their effects as men do in the providence which they exert on their own affairs; but pre-assuming in themselves the measures of the whole of things, and producing the essence of every thing from themselves, and also looking to themselves, they *lead and perfect* all things in a silent path, by their very being, and fill them with good.

Neither, likewise, do they produce in a manner similar to nature, energizing only by their very being, unaccompanied with deliberate choice, nor energizing in a manner similar to partial souls in conjunction with will, are they deprived of production according to essence; but they contract both these into one union, and they will indeed such things as they are able to effect by their very being, but by their very essence being capable of and producing all things, they contain the cause of production in their unenvying and exuberant will.

By what busy energy, therefore, with what difficulty, or with the punishment of what Ixion, is the providence either of whole souls, or of intellectual essences, or of the Gods themselves accomplished, unless it should be said, that to impart good in any respect is laborious to the Gods? But *that which is according to nature is not laborious to any thing*. For neither is it laborious to fire to impart heat, nor to snow to refrigerate, nor in short to bodies to energize according to their own proper powers. And prior to bodies, neither is it laborious to natures to nourish, or generate, or increase. For these are the works of natures. Nor again, prior to these, is it laborious to souls. For these indeed produce many energies from deliberate choice, many from their very being, and are the causes of many motions by alone being present. So that if indeed the communication of good is according to nature to the Gods, providence also is according to nature. And these things we must say are accomplished by the Gods with facility, and by their very being alone. But if these things are not according to nature, neither will the Gods be naturally good. For the good is the supplier of good; just as life is the source of another life, and intellect is the source of intellectual illumination. And every thing which has a primary subsistence in each nature is generative of that which has a secondary subsistence.

That however, which is especially the illustrious prerogative of the Platonic theology, I should say is this, that according to it, neither is the exempt essence of the Gods converted to secondary natures, through a providential care for things subordinate, nor is their providential presence with all things diminished through their transcending the whole of things with undefiled purity, but at the same time it assigns to them a separate subsistence, and the being unmingled with every subordinate nature, and also the being extended to all things, and the taking care of and adorning their own progeny. For the manner in which they *pervade through all things* is not corporeal, as that of light is through the air, nor is it divisible about bodies, in the same manner as in nature, nor converted to subordinate natures, in the same manner as that of a partial soul, but it is separate from body, and without conversion to it, is immaterial, unmingled, unrestrained, uniform, primary and exempt.

To Beauty:

No word, or sound, or mystic pose,
Nor image fair though we compose
The form from forms e'en more sublime,
And work with art through endless time,
Could of this mighty splendour say
The smallest thing about its way.
For soul astonished, quickened and faint,
Relieves herself from all constraint,
Full-fired by love's uprising heat
She strives to see the splendour's seat:
   Beauty, beauty, beauty proceeding,
To the Good eternally leading;
Lovely as the source of love,
Symmetry of all above,
Delicate beyond compare,
Splendid beauty every where.
Nectar of Gods, of angels and of men,
This soul is open for your form to illumine;
Be she filled with all virtue, and heaven's sacred fire,
Singing with her god the ancient praises of their sire.
Beyond another, beyond reproach, perfection's dazzling light;
Beyond the stars, both high and low, beyond the realms of night;
Beauty untold! Astonishing my eye,
In silence are you honoured, in wonder do I sigh.

The Good, the Wise, and the Beautiful

Proclus, Theology of Plato, Book I

XXI Socrates, in the *Phaedrus*, says that every thing divine is beautiful, wise, and good and he indicates that this triad pervades to all the progressions of the Gods. What therefore is the goodness, what the wisdom, and what the beauty of the Gods? With respect to the goodness of the Gods therefore, we have before observed, that it preserves and gives subsistence to the whole of things, that it every where exists as the summit, as that which fills subordinate natures, and as pre-existing in every order analogous to the first principle of the divine orders. For according to this all the Gods are conjoined with the one cause of all things, and on account of this primarily derive their subsistence as Gods. For in all beings there is not any thing more perfect than the good, and the Gods. To the most excellent of beings therefore, and which are in every respect perfect, the best and most perfect of things is adapted.

XXII But in the *Philebus*, Plato delivers to us the three most principal elements of *The Good, viz.* the *desirable, the sufficient*, and *the perfect*. For it is necessary that it should convert all things to itself, and fill all things, and that it should be in no respect deficient, and should not diminish its exuberance.

Let no one therefore conceive the desirable to be such as that which is frequently extended in sensibles as the object of appetite. For such is apparent beauty. Nor let him suppose it to be such as is indeed able to energize upon and excite to itself the natures which are able to participate it, but which at the same time may be apprehended by intelligence, and is educed by us according to a projecting energy, and an adhesion of the dianoetic power. For it is ineffable, and prior to all knowledge extends to all beings. For all things desire *The Good*, and are converted to it.

But if it be requisite summarily to unfold the characteristic peculiarity of the desirable, as the supplier of light proceeds by his rays into secondary natures, converts the eye to himself, causes it to be solar-form, and to resemble himself, and through a different similitude conjoins it with his own fulgid splendour, thus also I think the desirable of the Gods allures and draws upward all things to the Gods in an ineffable manner by its own proper illuminations, being every where present to all things, and not deserting any order whatever of beings. Since even matter itself is said to be extended to this desirable, and through this desire is filled with as many goods as it is able to participate. It is therefore the centre of all beings, and all beings, and all the Gods have their essences, powers and energies about this. And the extension and desire of things towards this is *inextinguishable*. For all beings aspire after this desirable which is unknown and incomprehensible. Not being able therefore either to know or receive that which they desire, they dance round it, and are parturient and as it were prophetic with respect to it. But they have an unceasing and never-ending desire of its unknown and ineffable nature, at the same time that they are unable to embrace and embosom it. For being at once exempt from all things, it is similarly present to and moves all things about itself, and is at the same time by all of them incomprehensible. By this motion also and this desire it preserves all things. But by its unknown transcendency through which it surpasses the whole of things, it preserves its proper union unmingled with secondary natures. Such therefore is *the desirable*.

But *the sufficient* is full of boniform power, proceeds to all things, and extends to all beings the gifts of the Gods. For we conceive such a sufficiency as this to be a power pervading and protending to the last of things, extending the unenvying and exuberant will of the Gods, and not abiding in itself, but unically comprehending the super-plenitude, the never-failing, the infinite, and that which is generative of good in the divine hyparxis. For the desirable being firmly established, and surpassing the whole of things, and arranging all beings about itself, the sufficient begins the progression and multiplication of all good, calls forth that which is primary in the uniform hyparxis of the desirable, by its own prolific exuberance, and by *the beneficent replenishings* which pervade to all things, and copiously produces and imparts it to every being.

It is owing to the sufficient therefore, that the stability of divine natures, and that which proceeds from its proper causes is full of goodness, and that, in short, all beings are benefited, abiding in, proceeding from, and being united to their principles, and essentially separated from them. Through this power therefore, the intellectual genera give subsistence to natures similar to themselves, souls desire to generate, and imitate the beings prior to souls, natures deliver their productive principles into another place, and all things possess, in short, the love of generation. For the sufficiency of the goodness of the Gods, proceeding from this goodness, is disseminated in all beings, and *moves all things* to the unenvying communication of good; intellect indeed to the communication of intellectual, but soul of psychical, and nature of natural good.

All things therefore abide through the desirable of goodness, and generate and proceed into second and third generations through the sufficient. But the third thing, *the perfect*, is convertive of the whole of things, and circularly collects them to their causes; and this is accomplished by divine, intellectual, psychical and physical perfection. For all things participate of conversion, since the infinity of progression is through this again recalled to its principles; and the perfect is mingled from the desirable and sufficient. For every thing of this kind is the object of desire, and is generative of things similar to itself. Or in the works of nature also, are not perfect things every where lovely and prolific through the acme of their beauty?

The desirable therefore establishes all things, and comprehends them in itself. *The sufficient* excites them into progressions and generations. And *the perfect* consummately leads progressions to conversions and convolutions. But through these three causes, the goodness of the Gods fixing the unical power and authority of its proper hypostasis in this triad, is the *primary* and *most principal fountain* and *vestal seat* of things which have any kind of subsistence whatever.

XXXIII   After this, *wisdom* is allotted the second order, being the intelligence of the Gods, or rather the hyparxis of their intelligence. For intelligence indeed, is intellectual knowledge; but the wisdom of the Gods is ineffable knowledge, which is united to the object of knowledge and the intelligible union of the Gods. But it appears to me that Plato especially surveyed this in the triad [of the beautiful, the wise and the good,] as may be inferred from the conceptions scattered about it in many places.

I say then that Diotima in the *Banquet* is of opinion that wisdom is *full* of that which is known, and that it neither seeks, nor investigates, but possesses the intelligible. Hence, she says, that no one of the gods philosophizes, nor desires to become wise; for a God is wise. Hence that which is philosophic is imperfect, and indigent of truth; but that which is wise is full and unindigent, and has every thing present which it wishes and desires nothing. But the desirable and the appetible are proposed to the philosopher.

Socrates, however, in the *Republic* considers that which is *generative of truth and intellect*, as affording an indication of wisdom, to our souls indeed the ascent to divine plenitude being accomplished through knowledge, but to the Gods intellect being present from the fullness of knowledge. For the progression in them is not from an imperfect habit to the perfect; but from a self-perfect hyparxis a power prolific of inferior natures proceeds. But in the *Theætetus* he indicates that *the perfective* of things imperfect, and that which calls forth concealed intelligence in souls, pertain to wisdom. For he says, it compels me to obstetrication, but prevents me from generating.

It is evident therefore, from these things, that the genus of wisdom is triadic. Hence it is *full* of being and truth, is *generative* of intellectual truth, and is *perfective* of intellectual natures that are in energy, and itself possesses a stable power. We must admit therefore, that these things pertain to the wisdom of the Gods. For this wisdom is full indeed of divine goodness, generates divine truth, and perfects all things posterior to itself.

XXIV In the next place let us consider the beautiful, what it is, and how it primarily subsists in the Gods. It is said therefore to be boniform beauty, and intelligible beauty, to be more ancient than intellectual beauty, and to be beauty itself, and the cause of beauty to all beings; and all such like epithets. And it is rightly said. But it is separate not only from the beauty which is apparent in corporeal masses, from the symmetry which is in these from psychical elegance, and intellectual splendour, but also from the second and third progressions in the Gods; and subsisting in the intelligible place of survey, it proceeds from this to all the genera of the Gods, and illuminates their superessential unities, and all the essences suspended from these unities, as far as to the apparent vehicles of the Gods.

As therefore through the first goodness all the Gods are boniform, and through intelligible wisdom they have a knowledge ineffable, and established above intellect, thus also, I think, through the summit of beauty, every thing divine is *lovely*. For from thence all the Gods derive beauty, and being filled with it, fill the natures posterior to themselves, exciting all things, agitating them with Bacchic fury about the love of themselves, and pouring supernally on all things the divine effluxion of beauty.

Such therefore, in short, is divine beauty, the supplier of divine hilarity, familiarity and friendship. For through this the Gods are united to and rejoice in each other, admire, and are delighted in communicating with each other, and in their mutual replenishings, and do not desert the order which they are always allotted in the distributions of themselves. Plato also delivers three indications of this beauty, in the *Banquet* indeed, denominating it the *delicate*; for the perfect and that which is most blessed, accedes to the beautiful through the participation of goodness. But he thus speaks of it in that dialogue: That which is truly beautiful, is delicate, perfect and most blessed." One of the indications therefore of the beautiful, is a thing of this kind, *viz. the delicate*. But we may assume another indication of it from the *Phædrus*, *viz. the splendid*. For Plato attributing this to the beautiful says: "It was then that we were permitted to see splendid beauty shining upon us etc." And afterwards he adds: "And arriving hither we apprehended it shining most manifestly through the clearest of the senses." And at last he says: "But now beauty alone has this allotment to be most splendid and most lovely." These two things therefore are to be assumed as indications of beauty. Another indication of beauty is this, that it is the object of love, which now also Plato appears to me to have called most lovely. And in many other places he shows that the amatory fury is conversant with the beautiful, defining, and in short, suspending love from the monad of beauty. "For love, says he, is conversant with the beautiful."

Because, therefore, beauty converts and moves all things to itself, causes them to energize enthusiastically, and recalls them through love, it is the *object of love*, being the leader of the whole amatory series walking on the extremities of its feet, and exciting all things to itself through desire and astonishment. But again because it extends to secondary natures plenitudes from itself, in conjunction with hilarity and divine facility, alluring, enflaming, and elevating all things, and pouring on them illuminations from on high, it is *delicate*, and is said to be so by Plato. And because it bounds this triad, and covers as with a veil the ineffable union of the Gods, swims as it were on the light of forms, causes intelligible light to shine forth, and announces the occult nature of goodness, it is denominated *splendid*, lucid and manifest. For the goodness of the Gods is supreme and most united; their wisdom is in a certain respect now parturient with intelligible light, and the first forms; but their beauty is established in the highest forms, is the luminous precursor of divine light, and is the first thing that is apparent to ascending souls, being more splendid and more lovely to the view and to embrace than every luciferous essence, and when it appears is received with astonishment.

This triad therefore filling all things, and proceeding through all things, it is certainly necessary that the natures which are filled should be converted to and conjoined with each of the three through kindred, and not through the same media. For of different things that are filled by this triad there is a different medium; and different powers are converted to a different perfection of the Gods. I think therefore, it is manifest to every one, and it is frequently asserted by Plato, that the cause which congregates all secondary natures to divine beauty, which familiarizes them to it and is the source of their being filled with it, and of their derivation from thence, is nothing else than *love*, which always conjoins according to the beautiful, secondary to the first Gods, and the more excellent genera, and the best of souls. But again, *truth* is certainly the leader to, and establishes beings in, divine wisdom, with which intellect being filled, possesses a knowledge of beings, and souls participating of this energize intellectually. For the full participation of true wisdom is effected through truth, since this every where illuminates intellective natures, and conjoins them with the objects of intellection, just as truth also is the first thing that congregates intellect and the intelligible. To those however who hasten to be conjoined with the good, knowledge and co-operation are no longer requisite, but collocation, a firm establishment and quiet are necessary, *viz. faith*.

XXV What therefore is it which unites us to the good? What is it which causes in us a cessation of energy and motion. What is it which establishes all divine natures in the first and ineffable unity of goodness. And how does it come to pass that every thing being established in that which is prior to itself according to the good which is in itself again establishes things posterior to itself according to cause? It is, in short, the *faith* of the Gods, which ineffably unites all the genera of the Gods, of dæmons, and of happy souls to *The Good*. For it is necessary to investigate *The Good* neither gnostically, nor imperfectly, but giving ourselves up to the divine light, and closing the eyes of the soul, after this manner to become established in the unknown and occult unity of beings. For such a kind of faith as this is more ancient than the gnostic energy, not in us only, but with the Gods themselves, and according to this all the Gods are united, and about one centre uniformly collect the whole of their powers and progressions.

If however it be requisite to give a particular definition of this faith, let no one suppose that it is such a kind of faith as that which is conversant with the wandering about sensibles. For this falls short of science, and much more of the truth of beings. But the faith of the Gods surpasses all knowledge, and according to the highest union conjoins secondary with first natures. Nor again, let him conceive a faith of a similar species with the celebrated belief in common conceptions; for we believe in common conceptions prior to all reasoning. But the knowledge of these is divisible, and is by no means equivalent to divine union; and the science of these is not only posterior to faith, but also to intellectual simplicity. For intellect is established beyond all science, both the first science, and that which is posterior to it. Neither, therefore, must we say that the energy according to intellect is similar to such a faith as this. For intellectual energy is multiform, and is separated from the objects of intellection through difference; and in short, it is intellectual motion about the intelligible.

But it is necessary that divine faith should be uniform and quiet, being perfectly established in the port of goodness. For neither is the beautiful, nor wisdom, nor any thing else among beings, so credible and stable to all things, and so exempt from all ambiguity, divisible apprehension and motion, as *The Good*. For through this intellect also embraces another union more ancient than intellectual energy, and prior to energy. And soul considers the variety of intellect and the splendour of forms as nothing with respect to that transcendency of *The Good* by which it surpasses the whole of things. And it dismisses indeed intellectual perception, running back to its own hyparxis; but it always pursues, investigates, and aspires after *The Good*, hastens as it were to embosom it, and gives itself to this alone among all things without hesitation. But why is it necessary to speak of the soul? For these mortal animals, as Diotima somewhere says, despise all other things, and even life itself and being, through a desire of the nature of *The Good;* and all things have this one immoveable and ineffable tendency to *The Good;* but they overlook, consider as secondary, and despise the order of every thing else. This, therefore, is the one secure port of all beings.

This also is especially the object of belief to all beings. And through this the conjunction and union with it is denominated faith by theologists, and not by them only, but by Plato likewise, (if I may speak what appears to be to be the case) the alliance of this faith with truth and love is proclaimed in the *Laws*. The multitude therefore are ignorant, that he who has a conception of these things, when discoursing about their contraries, infers the same thing with respect to the deviations from this triad. Plato then clearly asserts in the *Laws* that the lover of falsehood is not to be believed, and that he who is not to be believed is void of friendship. Hence it is necessary that the lover of truth should be worthy of belief, and that he who is worthy of belief should be well adapted to friendship. From these things therefore, we may survey divine truth, faith and love, and comprehend by a reasoning process their stable communion with each other. If, however, you are willing, prior to these things we will recall to our memory that Plato denominates that virtue fidelity which conciliates those that disagree, and subverts the greatest of wards, I mean seditions in cities. For from these things faith appears to be the cause of union, communion and quiet. And if there is such a power as this in us, it is by a much greater priority in the Gods themselves. For as Plato speaks of a certain divine temperance, justice and science, how is it possible that faith which connectedly comprehends the whole order of the virtues should not subsist with the Gods?

In short, there are these three things which replenish divine natures, and which are the sources of plenitude to all the superior genera of beings, *viz.* goodness, wisdom and beauty. And again, there are three things which collect together the natures that are filled, being secondary indeed to the former, but pervading to all the divine orders, and these are faith, truth and love. *But all things are saved through these*, and are conjoined to their primary causes; some things indeed, through the amatory mania, others through divine philosophy, and others through theurgic power, which is more excellent than all human wisdom, and which comprehends prophetic good, the purifying powers of perfective good, and in short, all such things as are the effects of divine possession.

The Two Principles After The One

Socrates: But let us begin cautiously, and endeavour to lay down right principles.

Protarchus: What principles do you mean?

Socrates: All things which are now in the universe let us divide into two sorts, or rather, if you please, into three.

Protarchus: You should tell us what difference between things it is, with respect to which you make that division.

Socrates: Some things which have been already mentioned let us reassume.

Protarchus: What things?

Socrates: God, we said, has exhibited *the infinite*, and also *the bound* of beings.

Protarchus: Very true.

Socrates: Let us take these for *two* of the species of things; and for a *third* let us take that, which is composed of those two mixed together. But I deserve, methinks, to be laughed at for pretending thus to distinguish things, and to enumerate their several species.

Protarchus: Why so, my good friend?

Socrates: A fourth kind appears to have been omitted by me.

Protarchus: Say, what?

Socrates: Of that commixture, the combination of the former two, consider the cause: and beside those three species, set me down this cause [that is, the Ineffable Principle of All Things] for a fourth.

Plato: The Philebus, from 23c

Proclus' Theology of Plato, Book III

III   Again therefore, the mystic doctrine concerning *The One* must be resumed by us, in order that proceeding from the first principle, we may celebrate the second and third principles of the whole of things.

  Of all beings therefore, and of the Gods that produce beings, one exempt and imparticipable cause pre-exists, - a cause ineffable indeed by all language, and unknown by all knowledge and incomprehensible, unfolding all things into light from itself, subsisting ineffably prior to, and converting all things to itself, but existing as the best end of all things. This cause therefore, which is truly exempt from all causes, and which gives subsistence unically to all the unities of divine natures, and to all the genera of beings, and their progressions, Socrates in the *Republic* calls *The Good*, and through its analogy to the sun reveals its admirable and unknown transcendency with respect to all intelligibles. But again, Parmenides denominates it *The One*. And through negations demonstrates the exempt and ineffable hyparxis of this one which is the cause of the whole of things. But the discourse in the epistle to Dionysius proceeding through enigmas, celebrates it as that about which all things subsist, and as the cause of all beautiful things. In the *Philebus* however, Socrates celebrates it as that which gives subsistence to the whole of things, because it is the cause of all deity. For all the Gods derive their existence as Gods from the first God. Whether therefore, it be lawful to denominate it the fountain of deity, or the kingdom of beings, or the unity of all unities, or the goodness which is generative of truth, or an hyparxis exempt from all these things, and beyond all causes, both the paternal and the generative, let it be honoured by us in silence, and prior to silence by union, and of the mystic end may it impart by illumination a portion adapted to our souls.

But let us survey with intellect the biformed principles proceeding from and posterior to it. For what else is it necessary to arrange after the union of the whole theory, than the duad of principles? What the two principles therefore are of the divine orders after the first principle, we shall in the next place survey. For conformably to the theology of our ancestors, Plato also establishes two principles after *The One*.

In the *Philebus* therefore, Socrates says, that God gives subsistence to *bound* and *infinity*, and through these mingling all beings, has produced them, the nature of beings, according to Philolaus subsisting from the connexion of things bounded, and things infinite. If, therefore, all beings subsist *from* these, it is evident that they themselves have a subsistence *prior* to beings. And if secondary natures participate of these mingled together, *these will subsist unmingled prior to the whole of things*. For the progression of the divine orders originates, not from things co-ordinated and which exist in others, but from things exempt, and which are established in themselves. As therefore *The One* is prior to things united, and as that which is passive to The One, has a second order after the imparticipable union, thus also the two principles of beings, prior to the participation of and commixture with beings, are themselves by themselves the causes of the whole of things. For it is necessary that bound should be prior to things bounded, and infinity prior to infinites, according to the similitude to *The One* of things which proceed from it. For again, if we should produce beings immediately after *The One*, we shall no where find the peculiarity of *The One* subsisting purely. For neither is being the same with *The One*, but it participates of *The One*, nor in reality is that which is the first *The One*; for, as has been frequently said, it is better than *The One*. Where therefore is that which is most properly and entirely one? Hence there is a certain one prior to being, which gives subsistence to being, and is primarily the cause of it; since that which is prior to it is beyond union, and is a cause without habitude with respect to all things, and imparticipable, being exempt from all things. If however this one is the cause of being, and constitutes it, there will be a power in it generative of being. For every thing which produces, produces according to its own power, which is allotted a subsistence between that which produces and the things produced, and is of the one the progression and as it were extension, but of the other is the pre-arranged generative cause. For being which is produced from these, and which is not *The One Itself*, but uniform, possesses its progression indeed from *The One*, through the power which produces and unfolds it into light from *The One*; but its occult union from the hyparxis of *The One*. This one therefore which subsists prior to power, and first pre-subsists from the imparticipable and unknown cause of the whole of things, Socrates in the *Philebus* calls *bound*, but he denominates the power of it which is generative of being, *infinity*. But he thus speaks in that dialogue, "God we said has exhibited the bound, and also the infinite of beings."

The first therefore and unical God, is without any addition denominated by him God; because each of the second Gods is participated by being, and has being suspended from its nature. But the first indeed, as being exempt from the whole of beings, is God, defined according to the ineffable itself, the unical alone, and superessential. But the bound and the infinite of beings, unfold into light that unknown and imparticipable cause; bound indeed, being the cause of stable, uniform, and connective deity; but the infinite being the cause of power proceeding to all things and capable of being multiplied, and in short, being the leader of every generative distribution. For all union and wholeness, and communion of beings, and all the divine measures, are suspended from the first bound. But all division, prolific production, and progression into multitude, derive their subsistence from this most principal infinity. Hence, when we say that each of the divine orders abides and at the same time proceeds, we must confess that it *stably abides* indeed, *according to bound*, but *proceeds according to infinity*, and that at one and the same time it has unity and multitude, and we must suspend the former from the principle of bound, but the latter from that of infinity. And in short, of all the opposition in the divine genera, we must refer that which is the more excellent to bound, but that which is subordinate to infinity.

For from these two principles all things have their progression into being, even as far as to the last of things. For eternity itself participates at once of bound and infinity; so far indeed, as it is the intelligible measure, it participates of bound; but so far as it is the cause of a never-failing power of existing, it participates of infinity.

And intellect, so far indeed as it is uniform, and whole, and so far as it is connective of paradigmatical measures, so far it is the progeny of bound. But again, so far as it produces all things eternally, and subsists conformably to the whole of eternity, supplying all things with existence at once, and always possessing its own power undiminished, so far it is the progeny of infinity.

And soul indeed, in consequence of measuring its own life, by restitutions and periods, and introducing a boundary to its own motions, is referred to the cause of bound; but in consequence of having no cessation of motions, but making the end of one period the beginning of the whole of a second vital circulation, it is referred to the order of infinity.

The whole of this heaven also, according to the wholeness of itself, its connexion, the order of its periods, and the measures of its restitutions, is bounded. But according to its prolific powers, its various evolutions, and the never-failing revolutions of its orbs, it participates of infinity. Moreover, the whole of generation, in consequence of all its forms being bounded, and always permanent after the same manner, and in consequence of its own circle which imitates the celestial circulation, is similar to bound. But again, in consequence of the variety of the particulars of which it consists, their unceasing mutation, and the intervention of the more and the less in the participations of forms, it is the image of infinity. And in addition to these things, every natural production, according to its form indeed, is similar to bound, but according to its matter, resembles infinity. For these are suspended in the last place from the two principles posterior to *The One*, and as far as to these the progression of their productive power extends. Each of these also is one, but form is the measure and boundary of matter, and is in a greater degree one. Matter however is *all things in capacity*, so far as it derives its subsistence from the first power. There, however, power is generative of all things. But the power of matter is imperfect, and is indigent of the hypostasis which is generative of all things according to energy.

Very properly therefore is it said by Socrates that all beings are from bound and infinity, and that these two intelligible principles primarily derive their subsistence from God. For that which congregates both of them, and perfects them, and unfolds itself into light through all beings is *The One* prior to the duad. And union indeed is derived to all things through that which is first; but the division of the two orders of things is generated from these primary causes, and through these is extended to the unknown and ineffable principle.

Let it therefore be manifest through these things, what the two principles of beings are, which become proximately apparent from *The One*, according to the theology of Plato.

The One and The Good

Plotinus, Ennead VI, ix, 4 & 6-11

The perception of the highest God is not effected by science, nor by intelligence, like other intelligibles, but by the presence of him, which is a mode of knowledge superior to that of science. .

How, therefore, can we speak of *The One*, and how can we adapt it to intellectual conception? Shall we say that this may be accomplished, by admitting that it is more transcendently one than the monad and a point? For in these, indeed, the soul taking away magnitude and the multitude of number, ends in that which is smallest, and fixes itself in a certain thing which is indeed impartible, but which was in a partible nature, and is in something different from itself. But *The One* is neither in another thing, nor in that which is partible. Nor is it impartible in the same way as that which is smallest. For it is the greatest of all things, not in magnitude, but in power. So that it is without magnitude in power. For the natures also which are [immediately] posterior to it, are impartible in powers, and not in bulk.

The principle of all things likewise must be admitted to be infinite, not because he is magnitude or number which cannot be passed over, but because the power of him is incomprehensible. For when you conceive him to be intellect or God, he is more [excellent] than these. And again, when by the dianoetic power you equalize him with *The One*, or conceive him to be God, by recurring to that which is most united in your intellectual perception, he even transcends these appellations. For he is in himself, nor is any thing accidental to him.

By that which is sufficient to itself also the unity of his nature may be demonstrated. For it is necessary that the principle of all things should be most sufficient both to other things, and to itself, and that it should also be most un-indigent. But every thing which is multitudinous and not one, is indigent; since consisting of many things it is not one. Hence the essence of it requires to be one. But *The One* is not in want of itself. For it is *The One*. Moreover, that which is many, is in want of as many things as it is. And each of the things that are in it, as it subsists in conjunction with others, and is not in itself, is indigent of other things; and thus a thing of this kind exhibits indigence, both according to parts and according to the whole.

If, therefore, it is necessary there should be something which is most sufficient to itself, it is necessary there should be *The One*, which alone is a thing of such a kind, as neither to be indigent with reference to itself, nor with reference to another thing. For it does not seek after any thing in order that it may be, nor in order that it may be in an excellent condition, nor that it may be there established. For being the cause of existence to other things, and not deriving that which it is from others, nor its happiness, what addition can be made to it external to itself? Hence its happiness, or the excellency of its condition, is not accidental to it. For it is itself [all that is sufficient to itself].

There is not likewise any place for it. For it is not in want of a foundation, as if it were not able to sustain itself. For that which is established in another thing is inanimate, and a falling mass, if it is without a foundation. But other things are established on account of *The One*, through which also they at the same time subsist, and have the place in which they are arranged. That, however, which seeks after place is indigent. But the principle is not indigent of things posterior to itself. The principle, therefore, of all things is unindigent of all things. For that which is indigent, is indigent in consequence of aspiring after its principle. But if *The One* was indigent of any thing it would certainly seek not to be *The One*; so that it would be indigent of its destroyer. Everything, however, which is said to be indigent, is indigent of a good condition, and of that which preserves it. Hence to *The One* nothing is good, and, therefore, neither is the wish for any thing good to it. But it is *super-good*. And it is not good to itself, but to other things, which are able to participate of it.

Nor does *The One* possess intelligence, lest it should also possess difference; nor motion. For it is prior to motion, and prior to intelligence. For what is there which it will intellectually perceive? Shall we say itself? Prior to intellection, therefore, it will be ignorant, and will be in want of intelligence in order that it may know itself, though it is sufficient to itself. It does not follow, however, that because *The One* does not know itself, and does not intellectually perceive itself, there will be ignorance in it. For ignorance takes place where there is diversity, and when one thing is ignorant of another. That, however, which is *alone* neither knows any thing, nor has any thing of which it is ignorant. But being one, and associating with itself, it does not require the intellectual perception of itself; since neither is it necessary, in order that you may preserve *The One*, to adapt to it an association with itself. But it is requisite to take away intellectual perception, an association with itself, and the knowledge of itself, and of other things. For it is not proper to arrange it according to the act of perceiving intellectually, but rather according to intelligence. For intelligence does not perceive intellectually, but is the cause of intellectual perception to another thing. Cause, however, is not the same with the thing caused. But the cause of all things is not any one of them. Hence neither must it be denominated that good which it imparts to others; but it is after another manner *The Good*, in a way transcending other goods.

If however, because it is none of these things, you become indefinite in your decision, in this case establish yourself in the above mentioned particulars, and from these [ascend to] and fix yourself in God. But for this purpose you must not extend the dianoetic power outwardly. For God is not in a certain place, so as to desert other things; but wherever any thing is able to come into contact with him, there he is present.

Hence, as in other things, it is not possible to perceive something intellectually, while understanding and attending to another thing, but it is necessary not to introduce any thing else to the object of intellectual vision, in order that the perceiver may be the thing itself which is perceived; - thus also here, it is not possible for the soul to perceive God, while it retains the impression of something else, and energizes according to that impression.

Nor again, is it possible for the soul while occupied and detained by other things to be impressed with the form of something contrary to them. But as it is said of matter, that it ought to be void of all qualities, in order that it may receive the impressions of all things; thus also, and in a much greater degree, it is necessary that the soul should become formless, in order that there may be no impediment to its being filled and illuminated by the first principle of things.

If, however, this be the case, it is requisite that the soul, dismissing all externals, should be entirely converted to its inmost recesses, and should not be called to any thing external, but should be unintellective of all things; and prior to this indeed, in inclination, but then also it should be without the perception of forms.

It is likewise necessary that the soul, being ignorant of herself, should dwell on the contemplation of God, and associating, and as it were sufficiently conversing with him, should announce, if possible, the conference which it there held to another; which Minos perhaps having accomplished, was on this account said to be the familiar of Jupiter. Calling to mind also this conference, he established laws which were the images of it, being filled through the contact with divinity with materials for the institution of laws. Or may we not say that the soul, if she wishes to abide on high, will consider political concerns as unworthy to be the subject of conference with deity? For this indeed will be the language of him who has seen much of divinity. *For, as it is said, God is not external to any one, but is present with all things, though they are ignorant that he is so.* For they fly from him, or rather from themselves. They are unable, therefore, to apprehend that from which they fly. And having destroyed themselves, they are incapable of seeking after another. For neither will a child, when through insanity he becomes out of himself, recognize his father. But he who knows himself, will also know from whence he was derived.

If, therefore, a certain soul has known itself at another time, it will also know that its motion is not rectilinear, but that its natural motion is as it were in a circle about a certain thing, not externally, but about a centre. The centre, however, is that from which the circle proceeds; and therefore such a soul will be moved about the source of its existence. It will also be suspended from this, eagerly urging itself towards that to which all souls ought to hasten. But the souls of the Gods always tend thither; and by tending to this they are Gods. For whatever is conjoined to this is a God. But that which is very distant from it, is a multitudinous man and a brute. Is, therefore, that in the soul which is as it were a centre, the object of investigation? Or is it necessary to think that it is something else, in which as it were all centres concur? This centre, however, and this circle are assumed by us according to analogy. For the soul is not a circle in the same way as a figure; but because an ancient nature is in it and about it. And because the soul is suspended from a thing of this kind, and in a still greater degree when it is wholly separated from the body.

Now, however, since a part of us is detained by the body; just as if some one should have his feet in the water, but with the rest of his body should be above it; - thus also being elevated by that part which is not merged in body, we are conjoined to that which is as it were the centre of all things; after the same manner as we fix the centres of the greatest circles in the centre of the sphere by which they are comprehended. If, therefore, the circles were corporeal and not psychical, they would be conjoined to the centre locally, and the centre being situated in a certain place, the circles would revolve about it. Since, however, these souls are themselves intelligible, and this centre is above intellect, it must be admitted that this contact is effected by other powers than those by which an intellective nature is adapted to be conjoined to the object of intellectual perception.

The contact, also, is greater than that by which intellect is present [with the intelligible] through similitude and sameness, and is conjoined with a kindred nature, nothing intervening to separate the conjunction. For bodies, indeed, are prevented from being united to each other; but incorporeal natures are not separated from each other by bodies. Hence, one is not distant from the other by place, but by *otherness* and difference. When, therefore, difference is not present, then the natures which are not different are present with each other.

The principle of all things, therefore, not having any difference, is always present; but we are present with it when we have no difference. And it indeed does not aspire after us, in order that it may be conversant with us; but we aspire after it, in order that we may revolve about it. We indeed perpetually revolve about it, but we do not always behold it. As a band of singers, however, though it moves about the coryphæus, may be diverted to the survey of something foreign to the choir [and thus become discordant], but when it converts itself to him, sings well, and truly subsists about him; - thus also we perpetually revolve about the principle of all things, even when we are perfectly loosened from it, and have no longer a knowledge of it. Nor do we always look to it; but when we behold it, then we obtain the end of our wishes, and rest [from our search after felicity]. Then also we are no longer discordant, but form a truly divine dance about it.

In this dance, however, the soul beholds the fountain of life, the fountain of intellect, the principle of being, the cause of good, and the root of soul. And these are not poured forth from this fountain, so as to produce in it any diminution. For it is not a corporeal mass; since if it were, its progeny would be corruptible. But now they are perpetual, because the principle of them abides with invariable sameness; not being distributed into them, but remaining whole and entire. Hence, they likewise remain, just as if the sun being permanent, light also should be permanent. For we are not cut off from this fountain, nor are we separated from it, though the nature of body intervening, draws us to itself. But we are animated and preserved by an infusion from thence, this principle not imparting, and afterwards withdrawing itself from us; since it always supplies us with being, and always will as long as it continues to be that which it is. Or rather, we are what we are by verging to it.

Our well-being also consists in this tendency. And to be distant from it is nothing else than a diminution of existence. Here, likewise, the soul rests, and becomes out of the reach of evils, running back to that place which is free from ill. And here also, she energizes intellectually, is liberated from perturbations, and lives in reality. For the present life, and which is without God, is a vestige of life, and an imitation of that life which is real. But the life in the intelligible world consists in the energy of intellect.

Energy also generates Gods, through a tranquil and quiet contact with the principle of all things. It likewise generates beauty, justice, and virtue. *For the soul being filled with deity, brings forth these.* And this is both the beginning and end to the soul. It is the beginning indeed, because she originates from thence; but it is the end, because *The Good* is there, and because when the soul is situated there, she becomes what she was before. For the good which is here, and in sensible concerns, is a lapse, a flight, and a defluxion of the wings of the soul. But that *The Good* is there, is indicated by the love which is connascent with the soul; conformably to which Love is conjoined in marriage with souls, both in writings and in fables. For since the soul is different from God, but is derived from him, she necessarily loves him, and when she is there she has a celestial love; but the love which she here possesses is common and vulgar. For in the intelligible world the celestial Venus reigns; but here the popular Venus, who is as it were meretricious. Every soul also is a Venus. And this the nativity of Venus, and Love who was born at the same time with her, obscurely signify.

The soul, therefore, when in a condition conformable to nature, loves God, wishing to be united to him, being as it were the desire of a beautiful virgin to be conjoined with a beautiful Love. When, however, the soul descends into generation, then being as it were deceived by [spurious] nuptials, and associating herself with another and a mortal Love, she becomes petulant and insolent through being absent from her father. But when she again hates terrene wantonness and injustice, and becomes purified from the defilements which are here, and again returns to her father, then she is affected in the most felicitous manner. And those indeed who are ignorant of this affection, may from terrene love form some conjecture of divine love, by considering how great a felicity the possession of a most beloved object is conceived to be; and also by considering that these earthly objects of love are mortal and noxious, that the love of them is nothing more than the love of images, and that they lose their attractive power because they are not truly desirable, nor our real good, nor that which we investigate.

In the intelligible world, however, the true object of love is to be found, with which we may be conjoined, which we may participate, and truly possess, and which is not externally enveloped with flesh. *He however who knows this, will know what I say,* and will be convinced that the soul has then another life. The soul also proceeding to, and having now arrived at the desired end, and participating of deity, will know that the supplier of true life is then present. She will likewise then require nothing farther; for on the contrary, it will be requisite to lay aside other things, to stop in this alone, and to become this alone, amputating every thing else with which she is surrounded.

Hence, it is necessary to hasten our departure from hence, and to be indignant that we are bound in one part of our nature, in order that with the whole of our [true] selves, we may fold ourselves about divinity, and have no part void of contact with him. When this takes place therefore, the soul will both see divinity and herself, as far as it is lawful for her to see him. And she will see herself indeed illuminated, and full of intelligible light; or rather, she will perceive herself to be a pure light, unburthened, agile, and becoming to be a God, or rather being a God, and then shining forth as such to the view. But if she again becomes heavy, she then as it were wastes away.

How does it happen, therefore, that the soul does not abide there? Is it not because she has not yet wholly migrated from hence? But she will then, when her vision of deity possesses an uninterrupted continuity, and she is no longer impeded or disturbed in her intuition by the body. That however which sees divinity, is not the thing which is disturbed, but something else; when that which perceives him is at rest from the vision. But it is not then at rest according to a scientific energy, which consists in demonstrations, in credibilities, and a discursive process of the soul. For here vision, and that which sees, are no longer reason, but greater than and prior to reason. And in reason, indeed, they are as that is which is perceived.

He therefore who sees himself, will then, when he sees, behold himself to be such a thing as this, or rather he will be present with himself thus disposed, and becoming simple, will perceive himself to be a thing of this kind. Perhaps, however, neither must it be said that he sees, but that he is the thing seen; if it is necessary to call these two things, *i.e.* the perceiver and the thing perceived. But both are one; though it is bold to assert this. Then, indeed, the soul neither sees, nor distinguishes by seeing, nor imagines that there are two things; but becomes as it were another thing, and not itself. Nor does that which pertains to itself contribute any thing there. But becoming wholly absorbed in deity, she is one, conjoining as it were centre with centre. For here concurring, they are one; but they are then two when they are separate. For thus also we now denominate that which is another. Hence this spectacle is a thing difficult to explain by words. For how can any one narrate that as something different from himself, which when he sees he does not behold as different, but as one with himself?

This, therefore, is manifested by the mandate of the mysteries, which orders that they shall not be divulged to those who are uninitiated. For as that which is divine cannot be unfolded to the multitude, this mandate forbids the attempt to elucidate it to any one but him who is fortunately able to perceive it.

Since therefore, [in this conjunction with deity] there were not two things, but the perceiver was one with the thing perceived, as not being [properly speaking] vision but union; whoever becomes one by mingling with deity, and afterwards recollects this union, will have with himself an image of it. But he was also himself one, having with respect to himself no difference, nor with respect to other things. For then there was not any thing excited with him who had ascended thither; neither anger, nor the desire of any thing else, nor reason, nor a certain intellectual perception, nor, in short, was even he himself moved, if it be requisite also to assert this; but being as it were in an ecstasy, or energizing enthusiastically, he became established in quiet and solitary union, not at all deviating from his own essence, nor revolving about himself, but being entirely stable, and becoming as it were stability itself.

Neither was he then excited by any thing beautiful; but running above the beautiful, he passed beyond even the choir of the virtues. Just as if some one having entered into the interior of the adytum should leave behind all the statues in the temple, which on his departure from the adytum will first present themselves to his view, after the inward spectacle, and the association that was there, which was not with a statue or an image, but with the thing itself [which the images represent], and which necessarily become the second objects of his perception.

Perhaps, however, this was not a spectacle, but there was another mode of vision, *viz.* ecstasy, and an expansion and accession of himself, a desire of contact, rest, and a striving after conjunction, in order to behold what the adytum contains. But nothing will be present with him who beholds in any other way.

The wise prophets, therefore, obscurely signified by these imitations how this [highest] God is seen. But the wise priest understanding the enigma, and having entered into the adytum, obtains a true vision of what is there. If, however, he has not entered, he will conceive this adytum to be a certain invisible thing, and will have a *knowledge* of the fountain and principle, as the principle of things. But when situated there, he will *see* the principle, and will be conjoined with it, by a union of like with like, neglecting nothing divine which the soul is able to possess. Prior to the vision also it requires that which remains from the vision. But that which remains to him who passes beyond all things, is that which is prior to all things. For the nature of the soul will never accede to that which is entirely non-being. But proceeding indeed downwards it will fall into evil; and thus into non-being, yet not into that which is perfect nonentity. Running, however, in a contrary direction, it will arrive not at another thing, but at itself. And thus not being in another thing, it is not on that account in nothing, but is in itself. *To be in itself alone, however, and not in being, is to be in God.* For God also is something which is not essence, but beyond essence. Hence the soul when in this condition associates with him.

He, therefore, who perceives himself to associate with God, will have himself the similitude of him. And if he passes from himself as an image to the archetype, he will then have the end of his progression. But when he falls from the vision of God, if he again excites the virtue which is in himself, and perceives himself to be perfectly adorned; he will again be elevated through virtue, proceeding to intellect and wisdom, and afterwards to the principle of all things. *This, therefore, is the life of the Gods, and of divine and happy men, a liberation from all terrene concerns, a life unaccompanied with human pleasures, and a flight of the alone to the alone.*

The Gods

Proclus - Theology of Plato, Book I

XIII In the first place, therefore, we shall assume the things which are demonstrated in the *Laws*, and contemplate how they take the lead, with respect to the truth about the Gods, and are the most ancient of all the other mystic conceptions about a divine nature. Three things, therefore, are asserted by Plato in these writings;

> that there are Gods;
> that their providence extends to all things;
> and that they administer all things according to justice,
>> and suffer no perversion from worse natures.

That these then obtain the first rank among all theological dogmas, is perfectly evident. For what can be of a more leading nature, than the hyparxis of the Gods, or than boniform providence, or immutable and undeviating power? Through which they produce secondary natures uniformly, preserve themselves in an undefiled manner, and convert them to themselves. But the Gods indeed govern other things, but suffer nothing from subordinate natures, nor are changed with the variety of the things to which their providence extends. We shall learn, however, how these things are defined according to nature, if we endeavour to embrace by a reasoning process the scientific method of Plato about each of them; and prior to these, survey by what irrefragable arguments he proves that there are Gods; and thus afterwards consider such problems as are conjoined with this dogma.

Of all beings, therefore, it is necessary that some should move only, but that others should be moved only, and that the natures situated between these, should both move and be moved. And with respect to these last it is necessary, either that they should move others being themselves moved by others, or that they should be self-motive.

These four hypostases likewise, are necessarily placed in an orderly series, one after another; that which is moved only and suffers, depending on other primary causes; that which moves others, and is at the same time moved, being prior to this; that which is self-motive, and which is beyond that which both moves and is moved, beginning from itself, and through its own motion imparting the representation of being moved, to other things; and that which is immoveable, preceding whatever participates either producing or passive motion. For every thing self-motive, in consequence of possessing its perfection in a transition and interval of life, depends on another more ancient cause, which always subsists according to sameness, and in a similar manner, and whose life is not in time, but in eternity. For time is an image of eternity.

If, therefore, all things which are moved by themselves, are moved according to time, but the eternal form of motion is above that which is carried in time, the self-motive nature will be second in order, and not the first of beings. But that which moves others, and is moved by others, must necessarily be suspended from a self-motive nature: and not this alone, but likewise every alter-motive fabrication, as the Athenian guest demonstrates. For if all things, says he, should stand still, unless self-motive natures had a subsistence among things, there would be no such thing as that which is first moved. For that which is immoveable, is by no means naturally adapted to be moved, nor will there then be that which is first moved; but the alter-motive nature is indigent of another moving power.

The self-motive nature, therefore, alone, as beginning from its own energy, will move both itself and others in a secondary manner. For a thing of this kind imparts the power of being moved to alter-motive natures, in the same manner as an immoveable nature imparts a motive power to all beings. In the third place, that which is moved only, must first of all be suspended from things moved by another, but moving others. For it is necessary, both that other things, and the series of things moved, which extends in an orderly manner from on high to the last of things, should be filled with their proper media.

All bodies, therefore, belong to those things which are naturally moved only, and are passive. For they are productive of nothing, on account of possessing an hypostasis endued with interval, and participating of magnitude and bulk; since every thing productive and motive of others, naturally produces and moves, by employing an incorporeal power.

But of incorporeal natures, some are divisible about bodies, but others are exempt from such a division about the last of things. Those incorporeals, therefore, which are divisible about the bulks of bodies, whether they subsist in qualities, or in material forms, belong to the number of things moved by another, but at the same time moving others. For these, because they possess an incorporeal allotment, participate of a motive power; but because they are divided about bodies, are deprived of the power of verging to themselves, are divided together with their subjects, and are full of sluggishness from these, they are indigent of a motive nature which is not borne along in a foreign seat, but possesses an hypostasis in itself.

Where, therefore, shall we obtain that which moves itself? For things extended into natures possessing bulk and interval, or which are divided in these, and subsist inseparably about them, must necessarily either be moved only, or be motive through others. But it is necessary, as we have before observed, that a self-motive nature should be prior to these, which is perfectly established in itself, and not in others, and which fixes its energies in itself, and not in things different from itself. There is, therefore, another certain nature exempt from bodies, both in the heavens and in these very mutable elements, from which bodies primarily derive the power of being moved.

Hence, if it be requisite to discover what such an essence as this is, (rightly following Socrates, and considering what the end of things is,) which by being present to alter-motive natures, imparts to them a representation of self-motion, to which of the above mentioned natures shall we ascribe the power of things being moved from themselves? For all inanimate natures are alone alter-motive, and whatever they suffer, they are adapted to suffer, through a certain power externally moving and compelling. It remains, therefore, that animated natures must possess this representation, and that they are self-motive in a secondary degree, but that the soul which is in them, primarily moves itself, and is moved by itself, and that through a power derived from itself as it imparts life to bodies, so likewise it extends to them from itself a representation of being moved by themselves.

If, therefore, the self-motive essence is more ancient than alter-motive natures, but soul is primarily self-motive, from which the image of self-motion is imparted to bodies, soul will be beyond bodies, and the motion of every body, will be the progeny of soul, and of the motion it contains. Hence it is necessary that the whole heaven and all the bodies it contains possessing various motions, and being moved with these different motions, according to nature (for a circulation is natural to every body of this kind) should have ruling souls, which are essentially more ancient than bodies, and which are moved in themselves, and supernally illuminate these with the power of being moved.

It is necessary, therefore, that these souls which dispose in an orderly manner the whole world and the parts it contains, and who impart to every thing corporeal which is of itself destitute of life, the power of being moved, inspiring it, for this purpose, with the cause of motion, should either move all things conformably to reason, or after a contrary manner, which it is not lawful to assert.

But if indeed, this world and every thing in it which is disposed in an orderly manner, and is moved equally and perpetually according to nature, as is demonstrated, partly in the mathematical disciplines, and partly in physical discussions, is suspended from an irrational soul, which moving itself moves also other things, neither the order of the periods, nor the motion which is bounded by one reason, nor the position of bodies, nor any other or those things which are generated according to nature, will have a stable cause, and which is able to distribute every thing in an orderly manner, and according to an invariable sameness of subsistence. For every thing irrational is naturally adapted to be adorned by something different from itself, and is indefinite and unadorned in its own nature. But to commit all heaven to a thing of this kind, and a circulation revolving according to reason, and with an invariable sameness, is, by no means adapted, either to the nature of things, or to our undisciplined conceptions.

If however, an intellectual soul, and which employs reason, governs all things, and if every thing which is moved with a perpetual lation, is governed by a soul of this kind, and there is no one of the wholes in the universe destitute of soul (for no body is honourable if deprived of such a power as this, as Theophrastus somewhere says) if this be the case, whether does it possess this intellectual, perfect, and beneficent power, according to *participation*, or according to *essence*? For if, according to essence, it is necessary that every soul should be of this kind, since each according to its own nature is self-motive. But if, according to participation, there will be another intellect subsisting in energy, more ancient than soul, which *essentially* possesses intellection, and by its very being pre-assumes in itself the uniform knowledge of wholes; since it is also necessary that the soul which is essentialized according to reason, should possess that which pertains to intellect through *participation*, and that the intellectual nature should be twofold; the one subsisting primarily in a divine intellect itself; but the other, which proceeds from this, subsisting secondarily in soul.

To which, you may add, if you please, the presence of intellectual illumination in body. For whence is the whole of this heaven either spherical or moved in a circle, and whence does it revolve with a sameness of circulation according to one definite order? For how could it always be allotted the same idea and power immutably according to nature, if it did not participate of specific formation according to intellect? For, soul, indeed, is the supplier of motion; but the cause of a firm establishment, and that which reduces the unstable mutation of things that are moved, into sameness, and also a life which is bounded by one reason, and a circulation which subsists with invariable sameness, will evidently be superior to soul.

Body, therefore, and the whole of this sensible nature belong to things which are *alter-motive*. But soul is *self-motive*, binding in itself all corporeal motions; and prior to this is intellect which is *immoveable*. Let no one, however, suppose that I assert this immobility of intellect to resemble that which is sluggish, destitute of life, and without respiration, but that it is the *leading cause* of all motion, and the *fountain*, if you are willing so to denominate it, of all life, both of that which is converted to itself, and of that which has its hypostasis in other things.

Through these causes also, the world is denominated by Timæus, *an animal endued with soul and intellect*; being called by him an animal according to its own nature, and the life pervading to it from soul, and which is distributed about it, but animated or endued with soul, according to the presence of a divine soul in it, and endued with intellect, according to intellectual domination. For the supply of life, the government of soul, and the participation of intellect connect and contain the whole of heaven.

If, however, this intellect is essentially intellect, since Timæus indicating that the *essence of intellect is the same with its intellection*, denominates it divine; for he says, that soul receiving a divine intellect led an upright and wise life; if, therefore, this be the case, it is necessary that the whole world should be suspended from its divinity, and that motion indeed should be present to this universe from *soul*, but that its perpetual permanency and sameness of subsistence should be derived from *intellect*, and that its one union, the conspiration in it and sympathy, and its all-perfect measure should originate from that *unity*, from which intellect is uniform, soul is one, every being is whole and perfect according to its own nature, and every thing secondary together with perfection in its own proper nature, participates of another more excellent peculiarity, from an order which is always established above it. For that which is corporeal being alter-motive, derives from soul the representation of self-motive power, and is through it an animal.

But soul being self-motive participates of a life according to intellect, and energizing according to time, possesses a never-ceasing energy, and an ever-vigilant life from its proximity to intellect. And intellect possessing its life in eternity, always subsisting essentially in energy, and fixing all its stable intellection at once in intellect, is entirely deific through the cause prior to itself. For it has twofold energies as Plotinus says, some as intellect, but others as being inebriated with nectar. And elsewhere he observes, that this intellect, by that which is prior to itself and is not intellect, is a god; in the same manner as soul, by its summit which is above soul, is intellect; and as body, by the power which is prior to body, is soul.

All things therefore, as we have said, are suspended from *The One* through intellect and soul as media. And intellect indeed has the form of unity; but soul has the form of intellect; and the body of the world is vital. *But every thing is conjoined with that which is prior to itself.* And of natures posterior to these, one in a more proximate, but the other in a more remote degree, enjoys that which is divine.

And divinity, indeed, is prior to intellect, being primarily carried in an intellectual nature; but intellect is most divine, as being deified prior to other things; and soul is divine, so far as it requires an intellectual medium. But the body which participates of a soul of this kind, so far as body indeed, is also itself divine; for the illumination of divine light pervades supernally as far as to the last dependencies; yet it is not simply divine; but soul, by looking to intellect, and living from itself, is primarily divine.

My reasoning is also the same about each of the whole spheres, and about the bodies they contain. For all these imitate the whole heaven, since these likewise have a perpetual allotment; and with respect to the sublunary elements, they have not entirely an essential mutation, but they abide in the universe according to their wholenesses, and contain in themselves partial animals. For every wholeness has posterior to itself more partial essences.

As, therefore, in the heavens, the number of the stars proceeds together with the whole spheres, and as in the earth the multitude of partial terrestrial animals subsists together with their wholeness, thus also it appears to me to be necessary that in the wholes which have an intermediate subsistence, each element should be filled up with appropriate numbers. For how in the extremes can wholes which subsist prior to parts, be arranged together with parts, unless there is the same analogy of them in the intermediate natures?

But if each of the spheres is an animal, and is always established after the same manner, and gives completion to the universe, as possessing life indeed, it will always primarily participate of soul, but as preserving its own order immutable in the world, it will be comprehended by intellect, and as one and a whole, and the leader and ruler of its proper parts, it will be illuminated by divine union.

Not only the universe, therefore, but each also of its perpetual parts is animated and endued with intellect, and as much as possible is similar to the universe. For each of these parts is a universe with respect to its kindred multitude. In short, there is indeed one corporeal-formed wholeness of the universe, but there are many others under this, depending on this one; there is one soul of the universe, and after this, other souls, together with this disposing in an orderly manner the whole parts of the universe with undefiled purity; one intellect, and an intellectual number under this, participated by these souls; and one god who connectedly contains at once all mundane and supermundane natures, and a multitude of other gods, who distribute intellectual essences, and the souls suspended from these, and all the parts of the world.

For it is not to be supposed that each of the productions of nature is generative of things similar to itself, but that wholes and the first of mundane beings should not in a much greater degree extend in themselves the paradigm of a generation of this kind. For the similar is more allied, and more naturally adapted to the reason of cause than the dissimilar, in the same manner as the same than the different, and bound than the infinite.

These things, however, we shall accurately survey in what follows. But we shall now direct our attention to the second of the things demonstrated in the *Laws*, *viz.* that the Gods providentially attend at once to wholes and parts, and shall summarily discuss the irreprehensible conception of Plato about *the providence of the Gods*.

XIV From what has been said, therefore, it is evident to every one, that the Gods being the causes of all motion, some of them are *essential* and *vivific*, according to a self-motive, self-vital, and self-energetic power. But others of them are *intellectual*, and excite by their very being all secondary natures to the perfection of life, according to the fountain and principle of all second and third progressions of motion. And others are *unical*, or characterized by unity, deifying by participation all the whole genera of themselves, according to a primary, all-perfect, and unknown power of energy, and who are the leaders of one kind of motion, but are not the principle of another. But again others supply to secondary natures motion according to place or quality, but are essentially the causes of motion to themselves. For every thing which is the cause of essence to other things is much prior to this the cause to itself of its own proper energies and perfection.

Farther still, that which is self-motive is again the principle of motion, and being and life are imparted by soul to every thing in the world, and not local motion only and the other kinds of motion, but the progression into being is from soul, and by a much greater priority from an intellectual essence, which binds to itself the life of self-motive natures and precedes according to cause all temporaral energy. And in a still greater degree do motion, being, and life proceed from a unical hyparxis, which connectedly contains intellect and soul, is the source of *total good*, and proceeds as far as to the last of things. For of life indeed, not all the parts of the world are capable of participating, nor of intellect and a gnostic power; but of *The One* all things participate, as far as to matter itself, both wholes and parts, things which subsist according to nature, and the contraries to these; and there is not any thing which is deprived of a cause of this kind, nor can any thing ever participate of being, if it is deprived of *The One*.

If, therefore, the Gods produce all things, and contain all things, in the unknown comprehensions of themselves, how is it possible there should not be a providence of all things in these comprehensions, pervading supernally as far as to the most partial natures? For it is every where fit that offspring should enjoy the providential care of their causes. But all alter-motive are the progeny of self-motive natures. And things which subsist in time, either in the whole of time, or in a part of it, are the effects of eternal natures; because that which always is, is the cause of that which sometimes exists. And divine and unical genera, as they give subsistence to all multiplied natures, precede them in existence.

In short, there is no essence, or multitude of powers, which is not allotted its generation from *The One*. It is necessary, therefore, that all these should be partakers of the providence of preceding causes, being vivified indeed from the psychical gods, and circulating according to temporal periods; and participating of sameness and at the same time a stable condition of forms from the intellectual gods; but receiving into themselves the presence of union, of measure, and of the distribution of good from the first Gods. It is necessary, therefore, either that the Gods should know that a providential care of their own offspring is natural to them, and should not only give subsistence to secondary beings, and supply them with life, essence and union, but also previously comprehend in themselves the primary cause of the goods they contain, or, which it is not lawful to assert, that being Gods, they are ignorant of what is proper and fit.

For what ignorance can there be of beautiful things, with those who are the causes of beauty, or of things good, with those who are allotted an hyparxis defined by the nature of *The Good?* But if they are ignorant, neither do souls govern the universe according to intellect, nor are intellects carried in souls as in a vehicle, nor prior to these do the unities of the Gods contractedly comprehend in themselves all knowledge, which we have acknowledged they do through the former demonstrations.

If, therefore, they are not deprived of knowledge, being the fathers, leaders and governors of every thing in the world, and to them as being such a providential care of the things governed by, and following them, and generated by them, pertains, whether shall we say that they knowing the law which is according to nature, accomplish this law, or that through imbecility they are deprived of a providential attention to their possessions or progeny, for it is of no consequence as to the present discussion which of these two appellations you are willing to adopt? For if through want of power they neglect the superintendence of wholes, what is the cause of this want of power? For they do not move things externally, nor are other things indeed the causes of essence, but they assume the government of the things they have produced, but they rule over all things as if from the stern of a ship, themselves supplying being, themselves containing the measures of life, and themselves distributing to things their respective energies.

Whether also, are they unable to provide at once for all things, or they do not leave each of the parts destitute of their providential care? And if they are not curators of every thing in the world, whether do they providentially superintend greater things, but neglect such as are less? Or do they pay attention to the less, but neglect to take care of the greater? For if we deprive them of a providential attention to all things similarly, through the want of power, how, while we attribute to them a greater thing, *viz.* the production of all things, can we refuse to grant that which is naturally consequent to this, a providential attention to their productions? For it is the province of the power which produces a greater thing, to dispose in a becoming manner that which is less. But if they are curators of less things, and neglect such as are greater, how can this mode of providence be right? For that which is more allied, and more similar to any thing, is more appropriately and fitly disposed by nature to the participation of the good which that thing confers on it.

If, however, the Gods think that the first of mundane natures deserve their providential care, and that perfection of which they are the sources, but are unable to extend their regard to the last of things, what is it which can restrain the presence of the Gods from pervading all things? What is it which can impede their unenvying and exuberant energy? How can those who are capable of effecting greater things, be unable to govern such as are less? Or how can those who produce the essence even of the smallest things, not be the lords of the perfection of them, through a privation of power? For all these things are hostile to our natural conceptions.

It remains, therefore, that the Gods must know what is fit and appropriate, and that they must possess a power adapted to the perfection of their own nature, and to the government of the whole of things. But if they know that which is according to nature, and this to those who are the generating causes of all things is to take care of all things, and an exuberance of power, - if, this be the case, they are not deprived of a providential attention of this kind.

Whether, also, together with what has been said, is there a will of providence in them? Or is this alone wanting both to their knowledge and power? And on this account are things deprived of their providential care? For if indeed knowing what is fit for themselves, and being able to accomplish what they know, they are unwilling to provide for their own offspring, they will be indigent of goodness, their unenvying exuberance will perish, and we shall do nothing else than abolish the hyparxis according to which they are essentialized. For *the very being of the Gods is defined by the good, and in this they have their subsistence.* But to provide for things of a subject nature, is to confer on them a certain good.

How, therefore, can we deprive the Gods of providence, without at the same time depriving them of goodness? And how if we subvert their goodness is it possible, that we should not also ignorantly subvert their hyparxis which we established by the former demonstrations? Hence it is necessary to admit as a thing consequent to the very being of the Gods that they are good according to every virtue. And again, it is consequent to this that they do not withdraw themselves from a providential attention to secondary natures, either through indolence, or imbecility, or ignorance. But to this I think it is also consequent that there is with them the most excellent *knowledge*, unpolluted *power*, and unenvying and exuberant *will*. From which it appears that they provide for the whole of things, and omit nothing which is requisite to the supply of good.

Let, however, no one think that the Gods extend such a providence about secondary things, as is either of a busy or laborious nature, or that this is the case with their exempt transcendency, which is established remote from mortal difficulty. For their blessedness is not willing to be defiled with the difficulty of administration, since even the life of good men is accompanied with facility, and is void of molestation and pain. But all labours and molestation arise from the impediments of matter.

If, however, it be requisite to define the mode of the providence of the Gods, it must be admitted that it is *spontaneous, unpolluted, immaterial,* and *ineffable.* For the Gods do not govern all things either by investigating what is fit, or exploring the good of every thing by ambiguous reasonings, or by looking externally, and following their effects as men do in the providence which they exert on their own affairs; but pre-assuming in themselves the measures of the whole of things, and producing the essence of every thing from themselves, and also looking to themselves, *they lead and perfect all things in a silent path, by their very being, and fill them with good.*

Neither, likewise, do they produce in a manner similar to nature, energizing only by their very being, unaccompanied with deliberate choice, nor energizing in a manner similar to partial souls in conjunction with will, are they deprived of production according to essence; but they contract both these into one union, and they will indeed such things as they are able to effect by their very being, but by their very essence being capable of and producing all things, they contain the cause of production in their unenvying and exuberant will.

By what busy energy, therefore, with what difficulty, or with the punishment of what Ixion, is the providence either of whole souls, or of intellectual essences, or of the Gods themselves accomplished, unless it should be said, that to impart good in any respect is laborious to the Gods? But *that which is according to nature is not laborious to any thing.* For neither is it laborious to fire to impart heat, nor to snow to refrigerate, nor in short to bodies to energize according to their own proper powers. And prior to bodies, neither is it laborious to natures to nourish, or generate, or increase. For these are the works of natures. Nor again, prior to these, is it laborious to souls. For these indeed produce many energies from deliberate choice, many from their very being, and are the causes of many motions by alone being present.

So that if indeed the communication of good is according to nature to the Gods, providence also is according to nature. And these things we must say are accomplished by the Gods with facility, and by their very being alone. But if these things are not according to nature, neither will the Gods be naturally good. For the good is the supplier of good; just as life is the source of another life, and intellect is the source of intellectual illumination. And every thing which has a primary subsistence in each nature is generative of that which has a secondary subsistence.

That however, which is especially the illustrious prerogative of the Platonic theology, I should say is this, that according to it, neither is the exempt essence of the Gods converted to secondary natures, through a providential care for things subordinate, nor is their providential presence with all things diminished through their transcending the whole of things with undefiled purity, but at the same time it assigns to them a separate subsistence, and the being unmingled with every subordinate nature, and also the being extended to all things, and the taking care of and adorning their own progeny. For the manner in which they pervade through all things is not corporeal, as that of light is through the air, nor is it divisible about bodies, in the same manner as in nature, nor converted to subordinate natures, in the same manner as that of a partial soul, but it is separate from body, and without conversion to it, is immaterial, unmingled, unrestrained, uniform, primary and exempt.

In short, such a mode of the providence of the Gods as this, must at present be conceived. For it is evident that it will be appropriate according to each order of the Gods. For soul indeed, is said to provide for secondary natures in one way, and intellect in another. But the providence of divinity who is prior to intellect is exerted according to a transcendency both of intellect and soul. And of the Gods themselves, the providence of the sublunary is different from that of the celestial divinities. Of the Gods also who are beyond the world, there are many orders, and the mode of providence is different according to each.

XV The third problem after these we shall connect with the former, and survey how we are to assume the unpervertible in the Gods, who perform all things according to *justice*, and who do not in the smallest degree subvert its boundary, or its undeviating rectitude, in their providential attention to all other things, and in the mutations of human affairs.

I think therefore, that this is apparent to every one, that every where that which governs according to nature, and pays all possible attention to the felicity of the governed, after this manner becomes the leader of that which it governs, and directs it to that which is best. For neither has the pilot who rules over the sailors and the ship any other precedaneous end than the safety of those that sail in the ship, and of the ship itself, nor does the physician who is the curator of the diseased, endeavour to do all things for the sake of any thing else than the health of the subjects of his care, whether it be requisite to cut them, or administer to them a purgative medicine. Nor would the general of an army or a guardian say that they look to any other end, than the one to the liberty of those that are guarded, and the other to the liberty of the soldiers. Nor will any other to whom it belongs to be the leader or curator of certain persons, endeavour to subvert the good of those that follow him, which it is his business to procure, and with a view to which he disposes in a becoming manner every thing belonging to those whom he governs.

If therefore we grant that the Gods are the leaders of the whole of things, and that their providence extends to all things, since they are good, and possess every virtue, how is it possible they should neglect the felicity of the objects of their providential care? Or how can they be inferior to other leaders in the providence of subordinate natures? Since the Gods indeed always look to that which is better, and establish this as the end of all their government, but other leaders overlook the good of men, and embrace vice rather than virtue, in consequence of being perverted by the gifts of the depraved.

And universally, whether you are willing to call the Gods leaders, or rulers, or guardians, or fathers, a divine nature will appear to be in want of no one of such names. For all things that are venerable and honourable subsist in them primarily. And on this account indeed, here also some things are naturally more venerable and honourable than others, because they exhibit an ultimate resemblance of the Gods. But what occasion is there to speak further on this subject? For I think that we hear from those who are wise in divine concerns paternal, guardian, ruling and pæonian powers celebrated.

How is it possible therefore that the images of the Gods which subsist according to nature, regarding the end which is adapted to them, should providentially attend to the order of the things which they govern, but that the Gods themselves with whom there is the whole of good, true and real virtue, and a blameless life, should not direct their government to the virtue and vice of men? And how can it be admitted, on this supposition, that they exhibit virtue victorious in the universe, and vice vanquished? Will they not also thus corrupt the measures of justice by the worship paid to them by the depraved, subvert the boundary of undeviating science, and cause the gifts of vice to appear more honourable than the pursuits of virtue? For this mode of providence is neither advantageous to these leaders, nor to those that follow them. For to those who have become wicked, there will be no liberation from guilt, since they will always endeavour to anticipate justice, and pervert the measures of desert. But it will be necessary, which it is not lawful to assert, that the Gods should regard as their final end the vice of the subjects of their providence, neglect their true salvation, and consequently be alone the causes of adumbrant good.

This universe also and the whole world will be filled with disorder and incurable perturbation, depravity remaining in it, and being replete with that discord which exists in badly governed cities. Though is it not perfectly impossible that parts should be governed according to nature in a greater degree than wholes, human than divine concerns, and images than primary causes?

Hence if men properly attend to the welfare of men in governing them, honouring some, but disgracing others, and every where giving a proper direction to the works of vice by the measure of virtue, it is much more necessary that the Gods should be the immutable governors of the whole of things. For men are allotted this virtue through similitude to the Gods.

But if we acknowledge that men who corrupt the safety and well-being of those whom they govern, imitate in a greater degree the providence of the Gods, we shall ignorantly at one and the same time entirely subvert the truth concerning the Gods, and the transcendency of virtue. For this I think is evident to every one, that what is more similar to the Gods is more happy than those things that are deprived of them through dissimilitude and diversity. So that if among men indeed, the uncorrupted and undeviating form of providence is honourable, it must undoubtedly be in a much greater degree honourable with the Gods. But if with them, mortal gifts are more venerable than the divine measures of justice, with men also earth-born gifts will be more honourable than Olympian goods, and the blandishments of vice than the works of virtue.

With a view therefore to the most perfect felicity, Plato in the *Laws* delivers to us through these demonstrations, *the hyparxis of the Gods, their providential care extending to all things*, and *their immutable energy*; which things, indeed, are common to all the Gods, but are most principal and first according to nature in the doctrine pertaining to them. For this triad appears to pervade as far as to the most partial natures in the divine orders, originating supernally from the occult genera of Gods. For a *uniform hyparxis*, a *power* which providentially takes care of all secondary natures, and an undeviating and immutable *intellect*, are in all the Gods that are prior to and in the world.

XVI Again, from another principle we may be able to apprehend the theological demonstrations in the *Republic*. For these are common to all the divine orders, similarly extend to all the discussion about the Gods, and unfold to us truth in uninterrupted connexion with what has been before said.

In the second book of the *Republic* therefore, Socrates describes certain theological types for mythological poets, and exhorts his pupils to purify themselves from those tragic disciplines, which some do not refuse to introduce to a divine nature, concealing in these as in veils the arcane mysteries concerning the Gods.

Socrates therefore, as I have said, narrating the types and laws of divine fables, which afford this apparent meaning, and the inward concealed scope, which regards as its end the beautiful and the natural in the fictions about the Gods, - in the first place indeed, thinks fit to evince, according to our unperverted conception about the Gods and their goodness, that they are the suppliers of all good, but the causes of no evil to any being at any time.

In the second place, he says that they are essentially immutable, and that they neither have various forms, deceiving and fascinating, nor are the authors of the greatest evil lying, in deeds or in words, or of error and folly. These therefore being two laws, the former has two conclusions, *viz.* that the Gods are not the causes of evils, and that they are the causes of all good. The second law also in a similar manner has two other conclusions; and these are, that every divine nature is immutable, and is established pure from falsehood and artificial variety.

All the things demonstrated therefore, depend on these three common conceptions about a divine nature, *viz.* on the conceptions about its *goodness, immutability* and *truth*. For the first and ineffable fountain of good is with the Gods; together with eternity, which is the cause of a power that has an invariable sameness of subsistence; and the first intellect which is beings themselves, and the truth which is in real beings.

XVII That therefore, which has the hyparxis of itself, and the whole of its essence defined in the good, and which by its very being produces all things, must necessarily be productive of every good, but of no evil. For if there was any thing primarily good, which is not God, perhaps some one might say that divinity is indeed a cause of good, but that he does not impart to beings every good.

If, however, not only every God is good, but that which is primarily boniform and beneficent is God, (for that which is primarily good will not be the second after the Gods, because every where, things which have a secondary subsistence, receive the peculiarity of their hyparxis from those that subsist primarily) - this being the case, it is perfectly necessary that divinity should be the cause of good, and of all such goods as proceed into secondary descents, as far as to the last of things. For as the power which is the cause of life, gives subsistence to all life, as the power which is the cause of knowledge, produces all knowledge, as the power which is the cause of beauty, produces every thing beautiful, as well the beauty which is in words, as that which is in the phænomena, and thus every primary cause produces all similars from itself and binds to itself the one hypostasis of things which subsist according to one form, - after the same manner I think the first and most principal good, and uniform hyparxis, establishes in and about itself, the causes and comprehensions of all goods at once.

Nor is there any thing good which does not possess this power from it, nor beneficent which being converted to it, does not participate of this cause. For all goods are from thence produced, perfected and preserved; and the one series and order of universal good, depends on that fountain.

Through the same cause of hyparxis therefore, the Gods are the suppliers of all good, and of no evil. For that which is primarily good, gives subsistence to every good from itself, and is not the cause of an allotment contrary to itself; since that which is productive of life, is not the cause of the privation of life, and that which is the source of beauty is exempt from the nature of that which is void of beauty and is deformed, and from the causes of this. Hence, of that which primarily constitutes good, it is not lawful to assert that it is the cause of contrary progeny; but the nature of goods proceeds from thence undefiled, unmingled and uniform.

And the divine cause indeed of goods is established eternally in itself, extending to all secondary natures, an unenvying and exuberant participation of good. Of its participants, however, some preserve the participation with incorruptible purity, receiving their proper good in undefiled bosoms, and thus through an abundance of power possess inevitably an allotment of goods adapted to them.

But those natures which are arranged in the last of the whole of things, entirely indeed enjoy according to their nature the goodness of the Gods; for it is not possible that things perfectly destitute of good should either have a being, or subsist at first; but receiving an efflux of this kind, they neither preserve the gift which pervades to them, pure and unmingled, nor do they retain their proper good stably, and with invariable sameness, but becoming imbecil, partial and material, and filled with the privation of vitality of their subject, they exhibit to order indeed, the privation of order, to reason irrationality, and to virtue, the contrary to it, vice.

And with respect indeed to the natures which rank as wholes, each of these is exempt from a perversion of this kind, things more perfect in them always having dominion according to nature. But partial natures through a diminution of power always diverging into multitude, division and interval, obscure indeed the participation of good, but substitute the contrary in the mixture with good, and which is vanquished by the combination. For neither here is it lawful for evil to subsist unmingled, and perfectly destitute of good; but though some particular thing may be evil to a part, yet it is entirely good to the whole and to the universe. For the universe is always happy, and always consists of perfect parts, and which subsist according to nature. But that which is preternatural is always evil to partial natures, and deformity, privation of symmetry, perversion, and a resemblance of subsistence are in these. For its proper perfection, but to the universe it is incorruptible and indestructible.

And every thing which is deprived of good, so far indeed as pertains to itself, and its own subsistence, is deprived of it through imbecility of nature; but it is good to the whole, and so far as it is a part of the universe. For it is not possible that either a privation of life, or deformity and immoderation, or in short privation can be inserted in the universe; but its whole number is always perfect, being held together by the goodness of wholes. And life is every where present, together with existence, and the being perfect, so far as each thing gives completion to the whole.

Divinity therefore, as we have said, is the cause of good; but the shadowy subsistence of evil does not subsist from power, but from the imbecility of the natures which receive the illuminations of the Gods. Nor is evil in wholes, but in partial natures, nor yet in all these. For the first of partial natures and partial intellectual genera are eternally boniform.

But the media among these, and which energize according to time, connecting the participation of the good with temporal mutation and motion, are incapable of preserving the gift of the Gods immoveable, uniform and simple; by their variety obscuring the simplicity of this gift, by their multiform its uniform nature, and by their commixture its purity and incorruptibility. For they do not consist of incorruptible first genera, nor have they a simple essence, nor uniform powers, but such as are composed of the contraries to these, as Socrates somewhere says in the *Phædrus.*

And the last of partial natures and which are also material, in a much greater degree pervert their proper good. For they are mingled with a privation of life, and have a subsistence resembling that of an image, since it is replete with much of non-entity, consists of things hostile to each other, and of circumstances which are mutable and dispersed through the whole of time, so that they never cease to evince in every thing that they are given up to corruption, privation of symmetry, deformity, and all-various mutations, being not only extended in their energies, like the natures prior to them, but being replete both in their powers and energies with that which is preternatural, and with material imbecility. For things which become situated in a foreign place, by co-introducing whole together with form, rule over the subject nature; but again receding to that which is partial, from their proper wholeness, and participating of partibility, imbecility, war and the division which is the source of generation, they are necessarily all-variously changed.

Neither, therefore, is every being perfectly good; for there would not be the corruption and generation of bodies, nor the purification and punishment of souls.

Nor is there any evil in wholes: for the world would not be a blessed god, if the most principal parts of which it consists were imperfect. Nor are the Gods the causes of evils, in the same manner as they are of goods; but evil originates from the imbecility of the recipients of good, and a subsistence in the last of things.

Nor is the evil which has a shadowy subsistence in partial natures unmingled with good. But this participates of it in a certain respect, by its very existence being detained by good. Nor in short, is it possible for evil which is perfectly destitute of all good to have a subsistence. For evil itself is even beyond that which in no respect whatever has an existence, just as the good itself is beyond that which is perfectly being.

Nor is the evil which is in partial natures left in a disordered state, but even this is made subservient to good purposes by the Gods, and on this account justice purifies souls from depravity. But another order of gods purifies from the depravity which is in bodies. All things however are converted as much as possible to the goodness of the Gods. And wholes indeed remain in their proper boundaries, and also the perfect and beneficent genera of beings. But more partial and imperfect natures are adorned and arranged in a becoming manner, become subservient to the completion of wholes, are called upward to the beautiful, are changed, and in every way enjoy the participation of the good, so far as this can be accomplished by them.

For there cannot be a greater good to each of these, than what the Gods impart according to measures to their progeny: But all things, each separately, and all in common, receive such a portion of good, as it is possible for them to participate.

But if some things are filled with greater, and others with less goods, the power of the recipients, and the measures of the distribution must be assigned as the cause of this. For different things are adapted to different beings according to their nature. But *the Gods always extend good, in the same manner as the sun always emits light.* For a different thing receives this light differently according to its order, and receives the greatest portion of light it is capable of receiving. For all things are led according to justice, and good is not absent from any thing, but is present to every thing, according to an appropriate boundary of participation. And as the Athenian guest says, all things are in a good condition, and are arranged by the Gods.

Let no one therefore say, that there are precedaneous productive principles of evil in nature, or intellectual paradigms of evils, in the same manner as there are of goods, or that there is a malefic soul, or an evil-producing cause in the Gods, nor let him introduce sedition and eternal war against the first good. For all these are foreign from the science of Plato, and being more remote from the truth wander into barbaric folly, and gigantic mythology. Nor if certain persons speaking obscurely in arcane narrations, devise things of this kind, shall we make any alteration in the apparent apparatus of what they indicate. But the truth indeed of those things is to be investigated, and in the mean time, the science of Plato must be genuinely received in the pure bosoms of the soul, and must be preserved undefiled and unmingled with contrary opinions.

XVIII In the next place, let us survey the *immutability* and *simplicity* of the Gods, what the nature of each of them is, and how both these appear to be adapted to the hyparxis of the Gods, according to the narration of Plato.

The Gods, therefore, are exempt from the whole of things. But filling these, as we have said, with good, they are themselves perfectly good; each of them according to his proper order possesses that which is most excellent; and the whole genus of the Gods is at once allotted predominance according to an exuberance of good.

But here again, we must oppose those who interpret in a divisible manner that which is most excellent in the Gods, and who say, that if the first cause is most excellent, that which is posterior to the first is not so. For it is necessary, say they, that what is produced should be inferior to that by which it is produced. And this indeed is rightly asserted by them. For it is necessary in the Gods, to preserve the order of causes unconfused, and to define separately their second and third progressions.

But together with a progression of this kind, and with the unfolding into light of things secondary from those that are first, that which is most excellent must also be surveyed in each of the Gods. For each of the Gods in his own characteristic peculiarity is allotted a transcendency which is primary and perfectly good. One of them indeed, that we may speak of something known, is allotted this transcendency, and is most excellent as possessing a prophetic power, another as demiurgic, but another as a perfector of works. And Timæus indicating this to us, continually calls the first demiurgus the best of causes. For the world, says he, is the most beautiful of generated natures, and its artificer is the best of causes; though the intelligible paradigm, and which is the most beautiful of intelligibles is prior to the demiurgus. But this is most beautiful and at the same time most excellent, as the demiurgic paradigm; and the maker and at the same time father of the universe is most excellent, as a demiurgic God.

In the *Republic* also, Socrates speaking of the Gods, very properly observes, that each of them being as much as possible most beautiful and most excellent, remains always with a simplicity of subsistence in his own form. For each of them being allotted that which is first and the summit in his own series, does not depart from his own order, but contains the blessedness and felicity of his own proper power. And neither does he exchange his present for a worse order; for it is not lawful for that which possesses all virtue to be changed into a worse condition; not does he pass into a better order. For where can there be any thing better than that which is most excellent? But this is present with each of the divinities according to his own order, as we have said, and also with every genus of the Gods.

It is necessary therefore that every divine nature should be established immutably, abiding in its own accustomed manner. Hence from these things the *self-sufficiency, undefiled purity*, and *invariable sameness of subsistence* of the Gods is apparent. For if they are not changed to a more excellent condition of being, as possessing that which is best in their own nature, they are sufficient to themselves, and are not in want of any good. And if they are not at any time changed to a worse condition, they remain undefiled, established in their own transcendencies. If also they guard the perfection of themselves immutably, they subsist always with invariable sameness. What the self-sufficiency therefore of the Gods is, what their immutability, and what their sameness of subsistence, we shall in the next place consider.

The world then is said to be self-sufficient, because its subsistence is perfect from things perfect, and a whole from wholes; and because it is filled with all appropriate goods from its generating father. But a perfection and self-sufficiency of this kind is partible, and is said to consist of many things coalescing in one, and is filled from separate causes according to participation.

The order of divine souls also, is said to be self-sufficient, as being full of appropriate virtues, and always preserving the measure of its own blessedness without indigence. But here likewise the self-sufficiency is in want of powers. For these souls have not their intellections directed to the same intelligibles; but they energize according to time, and obtain the complete perfection of their contemplation in whole periods of time. The self-sufficiency therefore of divine souls, and the whole perfection of their life is not at once present.

Again, the intellectual world is said to be self-sufficient, as having its whole good established in eternity, comprehending at once its whole blessedness, and being indigent of nothing, because all life and all intelligence are present with it, and nothing is deficient, nor does it desire any thing as absent. But this, indeed, is sufficient to itself in its own order, yet it falls short of the self-sufficiency of the Gods. For every intellect is boniform, yet is not goodness itself, nor primarily good; but each of the Gods is a *unity, hyparxis* and *goodness*.

The peculiarity however of hyparxis changes the progression of the goodness of each. For one divinity is a perfective goodness, another is a goodness connective of the whole of things, and another is a collective goodness. But each is simply a goodness sufficient to itself. Or it may be said, that each is a goodness possessing the self-sufficient and the all-perfect, neither according to participation, nor illumination, but by being that very thing which it is. For intellect is sufficient to itself by participation, and soul by illumination, but this universe, according to a similitude to a divine nature. The Gods themselves, however, are self-sufficient through and by themselves, filling themselves, or rather subsisting as the plenitudes of all good.

But with respect to the immutability of the Gods, of what kind shall we say it is? Is it such as that of a [naturally] circulating body? For neither is this adapted to receive any thing from inferior natures, nor is it filled with the mutation arising from generation, and the disorder which occurs in the sublunary regions. For the nature of the celestial bodies is immaterial and immutable. But this indeed is great and venerable, as in corporeal hypostases, yet it is inferior to the nature of the Gods. For every body possesses both its being, and its perpetual immutability from other precedaneous causes.

But neither is the impassive and the immutable in the Gods such as the immutability of souls. For these communicate in a certain respect with bodies, and are the media of an impartible essence, and of an essence divided about bodies.

Nor again is the immutability of intellectual essences equivalent to that of the Gods. For intellect is immutable, impassive, and unmingled with secondary natures, on account of its union with the Gods. And so far indeed as it is uniform, it is a thing of this kind; but so far as it is manifold, it has something which is more excellent, and something which is subordinate, in itself.

But the Gods alone having established their unions according to this transcendency of beings, are immutable dominations, are primary and impassive. For there is nothing in them which is not one and hyparxis. But as fire abolishes every thing which is foreign to it and of a contrary power, as light expels all darkness, and as lightning proceeds through all things without defilement, thus also the unities of the Gods unite all multitude, and abolish every thing which tends to dispersion and all-perfect division. But they deify every thing which participates of them, receiving nothing from their participants, and do not diminish their own proper union by the participation.

Hence also the Gods being present every where, are similarly exempt from all things, and containing all things are vanquished by no one of the things they contain; but they are unmingled with all things and undefiled.

In the third place, this world indeed is said to subsist with invariable sameness, so far as it is allotted an order in itself which is always preserved indissoluble. At the same time however, since it possesses a corporeal form, it is not destitute of mutation, as the Elean guest observes.

The psychical order likewise is said to obtain an essence always established in sameness; and this is rightly said. For it is entirely impassive according to *essence*; but it has *energies* extended into time, and as Socrates says in the *Phædrus*, at different times it understands different intelligibles, and in its progressions about intellect comes into contact with different forms.

Besides these also, much-honoured intellect is said both to subsist and to understand with invariable and perpetual sameness, establishing at once in eternity its essence, powers, and energies. Through the multitude however of its intellections, and through the variety of intelligible species and genera, there is not only an invariable sameness, but also a difference of subsistence in intellect. For *difference* there is consubsistent with *sameness*. And there is not only a wandering of corporeal motions, and of the psychical periods, but likewise of intellect itself, so far as it produces the intelligence of itself into multitude; and evolves the intelligible. For *soul indeed evolves intellect*, but *intellect the intelligible*, as Plotinus somewhere rightly observes, when speaking of the intelligible subjections. For such are the wanderings of intellect and which it is lawful for it to make.

If therefore we should say that a perpetual sameness of subsistence is primarily in the Gods alone, and is especially inherent in them, we shall not deviate from the truth, and we shall accord with Plato, who says in the *Politicus*, that an eternally invariable sameness of subsistence alone pertains to the most divine of all things. The Gods, therefore, bind to themselves the causes of a sameness of this kind, and guard with immutable sameness their proper hyparxis established according to the unknown union of themselves. And such is the immutability of the Gods, which is contained *in self-sufficiency, impassivity* and *sameness*.

XIX In the next place, let us consider what power the *simplicity* of the Gods possesses; for this Socrates adds in his discourse concerning a divine nature, not admitting that which is various, and multiform, and which appears different at different times, but referring to divinity the *uniform* and the *simple*.

Each of the divinities therefore, as he says, remains simply in his own form. What then shall we conclude respecting this simplicity? That it is not such as that which is defined to be one in number. For a thing of this kind is composed of many things, and abundantly mingled. But it appears to be simple so far as it has distinctly a common form.

Nor is it such as the simplicity which is in many things according to an arranged species or genus. For these are indeed more simple than the individuals in which they are inherent, but are replete with variety, communicate with matter, and receive the diversities of material natures.

Nor is it such as the form of nature. For nature is divided about bodies, verges to corporeal masses, emits many powers about the composition subject to it, and is indeed more simple than bodies, but has an essence mingled with their variety.

Nor is it such as the psychical simplicity. For soul subsisting as a medium between an impartible essence, and an essence which is divided about bodies, communicates with both the extremes. And by that which is multiform indeed in its nature it is conjoined with things subordinate, but its head is established on high, and according to this it is especially divine, and allied to intellect.

Nor again is the simplicity of the Gods such as that of intellect. For every intellect is impartible and uniform, but at the same time it possesses multitude and progression; by which it is evident that it has a habitude to secondary natures, to itself, and about itself. It is also in itself, and is not only uniform, but also multiform, and as it is said, is one many. It is therefore allotted an essence subordinate to the first simplicity.

But the Gods have their hyparxis defined in one simplicity alone, being exempt indeed from all multitude so far as they are gods, and transcending all division and interval, or habitude to secondary natures, and all composition. And they indeed are in inaccessible places, expanded above the whole of things, and eternally ride on beings. But the illuminations proceeding from them to secondary natures, being mingled in many places with their participants which are composite and various, are filled with a peculiarity similar to them.

Let no one therefore wonder, if the Gods being essentialized in one simplicity according to transcendency, various phantasms are hurled forth before the presence of them; nor, if they being uniform the appearances are multiform, as we have learnt in the most perfect of the mysteries. For nature, and the demiurgic intellect extend corporeal-formed images of things incorporeal, sensible images of intelligible, and of things without interval, images endued with interval.

For Socrates also in the *Phædrus* indicating things of this kind, and evincing that the mysteries into which souls without bodies are initiated are most blessed, and truly perfect, says, that they are initiated into entire, simple and immoveable visions, such souls becoming situated there, and united with the Gods themselves, but not meeting with the resemblances which are emitted from the Gods into these sublunary realms. For these are more partial and composite, and present themselves to the view attended with motion. But illuminated, uniform, simple, and, as Socrates says, immoveable spectacles exhibit themselves to the attendants of the Gods, and to souls that abandon the abundant tumult of generation, and who ascend to divinity pure and divested of the garments of mortality.

And thus much is concluded by us respecting the simplicity of the Gods. For it is necessary that the nature which generates things multiform should be simple and should precede what is generated, in the same manner as the uniform precedes the multiplied.

If, therefore, the Gods are the causes of all composition, and produce from themselves the variety of beings, it is certainly necessary that *The One* of their nature which is generative of the whole of things, should have its subsistence in simplicity. For as incorporeal causes precede bodies, immoveable causes things that are moved, and impartible causes all partible natures, after the same manner uniform intellectual powers precede multiform natures, unmingled powers, things that are mingled together, and simple powers, things of a variegated nature.

XX In the next place, let us speak concerning the *truth* which is in the Gods; for this in addition to what has been said is concluded by Socrates, because a divine nature is without falsehood, and is neither the cause of deception or ignorance to us, or to any other beings.

We must understand therefore, that divine truth is exempt from the truth which consists in words, so far as this truth is composite, and in a certain respect is mingled with its contrary, and because its subsistence consists of things that are not true. For the first parts do not admit of a truth of this kind, unless some one being persuaded by what Socrates asserts in the *Cratylus*, should say that these also are after another manner true.

Divine truth also is exempt from psychical truth, whether it is surveyed in opinions or in sciences, so far as it is in a certain respect divisible, and is not beings themselves, but is assimilated to and co-harmonized with beings, and as being perfected in motion and mutation falls short of the truth which is always firm, stable and of a principal nature.

Divine truth is likewise again exempt from intellectual truth, because though this subsists according to essence, and is said to be and is, beings themselves, through the power of sameness, yet again, through difference, it is separated from the essence of them, and preserves its peculiar hypostasis unconfused with respect to them.

The truth therefore of the Gods alone, is the undivided union and all-perfect communion of them. And through this the ineffable knowledge of the Gods, surpasses all knowledge, and all secondary forms of knowledge participate of an appropriate perfection. But this knowledge alone of the Gods contractedly comprehends these secondary forms of knowledge, and all beings according to an ineffable union. And through this the Gods know all things at once, wholes and parts, beings and non-beings, things eternal and things temporal, not in the same manner as intellect by the universal knows a part, and by being, non-being, but they know every thing immediately, such things as are common, and such as are particulars, though you should speak of the most absurd of all things, though you should speak of the infinity of contingencies, or even of matter itself.

If, however, you investigate the mode of the knowledge and truth of the Gods, concerning all things that have a subsistence in any respect whatever, it is ineffable and incomprehensible by the projecting energies of the human intellect; but is alone known to the Gods themselves.

And I indeed admire those Platonists that attribute to intellect the knowledge of all things, of individuals, of things preternatural, and in short, of evils, and on this account establish intellectual paradigms of these. But I much more admire those who separate the intellectual peculiarity from divine union. For *intellect is the first fabrication and progeny of the Gods.* These therefore assign to intellect whole and first causes, and such as are according to nature, and to the Gods a power which is capable of adorning and generating all things. For *The One* is every where, but whole is not every where. And of *The One* indeed matter participates and every being; but of intellect and intellectual species and genera, all things do not participate.

All things therefore are alone from the Gods, and real truth is with them who know all things unically. For on this account also, in oracles the Gods similarly teach all things, wholes and parts, things eternal, and such as are generated through the whole of time. For being exempt from eternal beings, and from those that exist in time, they contract in themselves the knowledge of each and of all things, according to one united truth.

If therefore any falsehood occurs in the oracles of the Gods, we must not say that a thing of this kind originates from the Gods, but from the recipients, or the instruments, or the places, or the times. For all these contribute to the participation of divine knowledge, and when they are appropriately co-adapted to the Gods, they receive a pure illumination of the truth which is established in them. But when they are separated from the Gods through inaptitude, and become discordant with them, then they obscure the truth which proceeds from them.

What kind of falsehood therefore can be said to be derived from the Gods, who produce all the species of knowledge? What deception can there be with those who establish in themselves the whole of truth? In the same manner, as it appears to me, the Gods extend good to all things, but always that which is willing and able receives the extended good, as Socrates says in the *Phædrus*. And a divine nature indeed is causeless of evil, but that which departs from it, and gravitates downwards, is elongated through itself; thus also, the Gods indeed are always the suppliers of truth, but those natures are illuminated by them, who are lawfully their participants. For the Elean wise man says, that the eye of the soul in the multitude, is not strong enough to look to the truth.

The Athenian guest also celebrates this truth which subsists primarily in the Gods; for he says that truth is the leader to the Gods of every good, and likewise of every good to men. For as the truth which is in souls conjoins them with intellect, and as intellectual truth conducts all the intellectual orders to *The One*, thus also the truth of the Gods unites the divine unities to the fountain of all good, with which being conjoined, they are filled with all boniform power. For every where the hyparxis of truth has a cause which is collective of multitude into one; since in the *Republic* also, the light proceeding from *The Good* and which conjoins intellect with the intelligible, is denominated by Plato truth. This characteristic property therefore, which unites and binds together the natures that fill and the natures that are filled, according to all the orders of the Gods, must be arranged as originating supernally and proceeding as far as to the last of things.

XXIX It now remains, I think, to speak of divine names. For Socrates in the *Cratylus* thinks fit to unfold in a remarkable degree the rectitude of names in divine natures. And Parmenides indeed, in the first hypothesis, as he denies of *The One* every thing else that is known, and all knowledge, so likewise he denies of it name and language. But in the second hypothesis, besides all other things he shows that this one may be spoken of and that it has a name. In short therefore, it must be admitted that the first, most principal and truly divine names are established in the Gods themselves. But it must be said that the second names, which are the imitations of the first, and which subsist intellectually, are of a dæmoniacal allotment.

And again, we may say that those names which are the third from the truth, which are logically devised, and which receive the ultimate resemblance of divine natures, are unfolded by scientific men, at one time energizing divinely, and at another intellectually, and generating moving images of their inward spectacles.

For as the demiurgic intellect establishes resemblances about matter of the first forms contained in himself, and produces temporal images of things eternal, divisible images of things indivisible, and adumbrated images as it were of true beings, - after the same manner I think the science that is with us representing intellectual production, fabricates resemblances of other things, and also of the Gods themselves, representing that which is void of composition in them, through composition; that which is simple, through variety; and that which is united, through multitude; and thus fashioning names, ultimately exhibits images of divine natures. For it generates every name as if it were a statue of the Gods.

And as the theurgic art through certain symbols calls forth the exuberant and unenvying goodness of the Gods into the illumination of artificial statues, thus also the intellectual science of divine concerns, by the compositions and divisions of sounds, unfolds the occult essence of the Gods. Very properly therefore, does Socrates in the *Philebus* say, that on account of his reverence of the Gods, he is agitated with the greatest fear respecting their names. For it is necessary to venerate even the ultimate echoes of the Gods, and venerating these to become established in the first paradigms of them.

"He who *simply believes in things which seem difficult to be known,* and which are of a dubious nature, *runs in the paths of abundance,* recurring to divine knowledge, and deific intelligence, through which all things become apparent and known. For all things are contained in the Gods."

Proclus

Section Two

The Universe of Being

Tim Addey

The Universe of Being

Chapter One

Plato's Theory of Ideas

In the first section we have taken extracts from various Platonists as a means for looking at reality primarily as a divine whole, emanated from *The One*, unfolded through the Gods, and finally manifesting its causal divinity in being. In this section I propose to look more closely at the resulting conditions of being, and while I will often return to consider its divine substratum, being and its various attributes will be my point of focus.

To begin, let us look at one of the most renowned passages of Plato – the allegory of the cave – in which our divine teacher urges us to consider the most basic question of metaphysics: what is real? In attempting to answer this question, the speaker, Socrates, must also deal with the problem of how we are to perceive reality. The extract is taken from the seventh book of *The Rupublic*,[8] and follows a passage in which Socrates had explained that *The One* (or *The Good*), as source of all, as utterly transcendent, as first power, as final goal, is best understood by seeing an analogy to the sun and its relation to our world.

> *Socrates*: Consider men as in a subterraneous habitation, resembling a cave, with its entrance expanding to the light, and answering to the whole extent of the cave. Suppose them to have been in this cave from their childhood, with chains both on their legs and necks, so as to remain there, and only be able to look before them, but by the chain incapable to turn their heads round. Suppose them likewise to have the light of a fire, burning far above and behind them; and that between the fire and the fettered men there is a road above. Along this road, observe a low wall built, like that which screens the stage of mountebanks on which they exhibit their wonderful tricks.
>
> *Glauco*: I observe it.

[8] Republic VII, 514a ff.

Socrates: Behold now, along this wall, men bearing all sorts of utensils, raised above the wall, and human statues, and other animals, in wood and stone, and furniture of every kind. And, as is likely, some of those who are carrying these are speaking, and others silent.

Glauco: You mention a wonderful comparison, and wonderful fettered men.

Socrates: But such, however, as resemble us; for, in the first place, do you think that such as these see any thing of themselves, or of one another, but the shadows formed by the fire, falling on the opposite part of the cave?

Glauco: How can they if through the whole of life they be under a necessity, at least, of having their heads unmoved?

Socrates: But what do they see of what is carrying along? Is it not the very same?

Glauco: Why not?

Socrates: If then they were able to converse with one another, do not you think they would deem it proper to give names to those very things which they saw before them?

Glauco: Of necessity they must.

Socrates: And what if the opposite part of this prison had an echo, when any of those who passed along spake, do you imagine they would reckon that what spake was any thing else than the passing shadow?

Glauco: Not I, by Zeus!

Socrates: Such as these then will entirely judge that there is nothing true but the shadows of utensils.

Glauco: By an abundant necessity.

Socrates: With reference then, both to their freedom from these chains, and their cure of this ignorance, consider the nature of it, if such a thing should happen to them. When any one should be loosed, and obliged on a sudden to rise up, turn round his neck, and walk and look up towards the light; and in doing all these things should be pained, and unable, from the splendours, to behold the things of which he formerly saw the shadows, what do you think he would say, if one should tell him that formerly he had seen trifles, but now, being somewhat nearer to reality, and turned toward what was more real, he saw with more rectitude; and so, pointing out to him each of the things passing along, should question him, and oblige him to tell what it were; do not you think he would be both in doubt, and would deem what he had formerly seen to be more true than what was now pointed out to him?

Glauco: By far.

Socrates: And if he should oblige him to look to the light itself, would not he find pain in his eyes, and shun it; and, turning to such things as he is able to behold, reckon that these are really more clear than those pointed out?

Glauco: Just so.

Socrates: But if one should drag him from thence violently through a rough and steep ascent, and never stop till he drew him up to the light of the sun, would he not, whilst he was thus drawn, both be in torment, and be filled with indignation? And after he had even come to the light, having his eyes filled with splendour, he would be able to see none of these things now called true.

Glauco: He would not, suddenly at least.

Socrates: But he would require, I think, to be accustomed to it some time, if he were to perceive things above. And, first of all, he would most easily perceive shadows, afterwards the images of men and of other things in water, and after that the things themselves. And, with reference to these, he would more easily see the things in the heavens, and the heavens themselves, by looking in the night to the light of the stars, and the moon, than by day looking on the sun, and the light of the sun.

Glauco: How can it be otherwise?

Socrates: And, last of all, he may be able, I think, to perceive and contemplate the sun himself, not in water, not resemblances of him, in a foreign seat, but himself by himself, in his own proper region.

Glauco: Of necessity.

Socrates: And after this, he would now reason with himself concerning him, that it is he who gives the seasons, and years, and governs all things in the visible place; and that of all those things which he formerly saw, he is in a certain manner the cause.

Glauco: It is evident, that after these things he may arrive at such reasonings as these.

Socrates. But what? when he remembers his first habitation, and the wisdom which was there, and those who were then his companions in bonds, do you not think he will esteem himself happy by the change, and pity them?

Glauco. And that greatly.

Socrates. And if there were there any honours and encomiums and rewards among themselves, for him who most acutely perceived what passed along, and best remembered which of them were wont to pass foremost, which latest, and which of them went together; and from these observations were most able to presage what was to happen; does it appear to you that he will be desirous of such honours, or envy those who among these are honoured, and in power? Or, will he not rather wish to suffer that of Homer, and vehemently desire

> As labourer to some ignoble man
> To work for hire . . . .

and rather suffer any thing than to possess such opinions, and live after such a manner?

Glauco. I think that he would suffer, and embrace any thing rather than live in that manner.

Socrates. But consider this further: If such a one should descend, and sit down again in the same seat, would not his eyes be filled with darkness, in consequence of coming suddenly from the sun?

Glauco. Very much so.

Socrates. And should he now again be obliged to give his opinion of those shadows, and to dispute about them with those who are there eternally chained, whilst yet his eyes were dazzled, and before they recovered their former state, (which would not be effected in a short time) would he not afford them laughter? and would it not be said of him, that, having ascended, he was returned with vitiated eyes, and that it was not proper even to attempt to go above, and that whoever should attempt to liberate them, and lead them up, if ever they were able to get him into their hands, should be put to death?

Glauco. They would by all means put him to death.

Socrates. The whole of this image now, friend Glauco, is to be applied to our preceding discourse: for, if you compare this region, which is seen by the sight, to the habitation of the prison; and the light of the fire in it, to the power of the sun; and the ascent above, and the vision of things above, to the soul's ascent into the intelligible place; you will apprehend my meaning, since you want to hear it. But God knows whether it be true. Appearances then present themselves to my view as follows. In the intelligible place, the idea of *The Good* is the last object of vision, and is scarcely to be seen; but if it be seen, we must collect by reasoning that it is the cause to all of everything right and beautiful, generating in the visible place, light, and its lord the sun; and in the intelligible place, it is itself the lord, producing truth and intellect; and this must be beheld by him who is to act wisely, either privately or in public.

So according to Plato, we must make a distinction between "this region, which is seen by the sight" and "the intelligible place" which is "above." In the former region the degree of reality is conditioned and dependent upon what is "above": shadows and echoes form appearances, which have some relation their stable causes. The region of sense flickers like shadows because all material things are in a state of *becoming* – continually rising into and falling out of existence. Those who devote themselves solely to the study of material things without acknowledging their dependence upon immaterial ideas and principles are, in reality, in a profound state of ignorance. In the intelligible place, beyond the cave, however is the true vision of the heavens – the vision of true causes. In other words, the philosopher must rise above the perception of the senses – which of themselves can only inform about material things – and find some way of perceiving the greater reality of intelligible things. This distinction between the ever-changing realm of materiality and the stable world of intelligible being, together with the challenge of this philosophical path is referred to again in the *Phaedo*[9] in these terms:

Socrates: But what with respect to the acquisition of wisdom? Is the body an impediment or not, if any one associates it in the investigation of wisdom? What I mean is this: Have sight and hearing in men any truth? or is the case such as the poets perpetually sing, that

We nothing accurate or see or hear?

Though if these corporeal senses are neither accurate nor clear, by no means can the rest be so: for all the others are in a certain respect more depraved than these. Or does it not appear so to you?

[9] The *Phaedo* 64d ff.

Simmias. Entirely so.

Socrates. When then does the soul touch upon the truth? for, when it endeavours to consider any thing in conjunction with the body, it is evidently then deceived by the body.

Simmias. You speak the truth.

Socrates. Must not, therefore, something of reality become manifest to the soul, in the energy of reasoning, if this is ever the case?

Simmias. It must.

Socrates. But the soul then reasons in the most beautiful manner, when it is disturbed by nothing belonging to the body, neither by hearing, nor sight, nor pain, nor any pleasure, but subsists in the most eminent degree, itself by itself, bidding farewell to the body, and, as much as possible neither communicating nor being in contact with it, extends itself towards real being.

Simmias. These things are so.

Socrates. Does not the soul of a philosopher, therefore, in these employments, despise[10] the body in the most eminent degree, and, flying from it, seek to become essentially subsisting by itself?

Simmias. It appears so.

Socrates. But what shall we say, Simmias, about such things as the following? Do we say that the *just itself* is something or nothing?

Simmias. By Jupiter, we say it is something.

Socrates. And do we not also say, that the *beautiful* and the *good* are each of them something?

Simmias. How is it possible we should not?

Socrates. But did you ever at any time behold any one of these with your eyes?

Simmias. By no means.

Socrates. But did you ever touch upon these with any other corporeal sense? (but I speak concerning all of them; as for instance, about magnitude, health, strength, and, in one word, about the essence of all the rest, and which each truly possesses.) Is then the most true nature of these perceived through the ministry of the body? or rather shall we not say, that whoever among us prepares himself to think dianoëtically[11] in the most

---

[10] The word *despise* here is used in its original meaning, "to look down upon".

[11] See the glossary on page 168.

eminent and accurate manner about each particular object of his speculation, such a one will accede the nearest possible to the knowledge of each?

Simmias: Entirely so.

Socrates: Will not he, therefore, accomplish this in the most pure manner, who in the highest degree betakes himself to each through his dianoëtic power, neither employing sight in conjunction with the dianoëtic energy, nor attracting any other sense, together with his reasoning; but who, exercising a dianoëtic energy by itself sincere, at the same time endeavours to hunt after every thing which has true being subsisting by itself separate and pure; and who in the most eminent degree is liberated from the eyes and ears, and in short from the whole body, as disturbing the soul, and not suffering it to acquire truth and wisdom by its conjunction? Will not such a man, Simmias, procure for himself real being, if this can ever be asserted of any one?

What our soul seeks to contemplate is, then, *real being* – or the things of the intelligible place – while the information received through our senses refers only to the appearances of material things which are themselves in a constant state of flux. Socrates is, of course, considering the soul in relation to its primary intellectual task – which is to understand the causal reality behind material existence; only as far as we do this, can we then bring order and beauty to that portion of the material world over which we have influence. A further demonstration of what Socrates has asserted here, is that whenever we are faced with a difficult intellectual problem, we seek uninterrupted quiet and a cessation of sense data in order to think through things – we often close our eyes, for example, in such circumstances. A little later (from 80b) in the dialogue Plato gathers together the various attributes of both real beings and their material counterparts.

Real Being	Things in process
divine	corporeal
immortal	not immortal
intelligible	non-intelligible
having a single form	multifarious
indissoluble	dissoluble
the same condition & nature	ever changing

Damascius in his commentary on this passage[12] systemises it in the following words:

"There are two kinds of forms, real-existents and things in process; secondly that the number and nature of what might be called the elements of each are the following:

Things that have true being are 'divine' because they are dependent of Gods before them. They are 'immortal' because their nature is eternal; for since they do not lack anything, neither can they ever lack life. They are 'intelligible' in the sense that they are capable of thought; this is proved by the contrasting attribute of things in process, 'non-intelligible'.[13] In the *Timaeus* the word is used in the same meaning. They 'have a single form' because they are form only and are simple forms, indivisible because of their unity. They are 'indissoluble' as a consequence of being indivisible, without parts and absolutely non-dimensional; for anything that is dissolved, is dissolved into its components. Existents as such are 'always of the same condition and quality'; for in that which is real in the proper and primary sense there neither was nor will be anything that is not; therefore they are entirely invariable.

Things in process are described by the narrower term 'human things'; elsewhere [*Laws* I 631b–d] Plato contradistinguishes the human as corporeal from the divine, inasmuch as the divine partiticipates in the Gods, whereas human nature on its lower level is participated by the body. Rather we should contrast the divine as the most completely united with the human as the most radically disintegrated.[14] They are all without exception 'not immortal'

---

[12] Damascius *Commentary on the Phaedo*, I, 312-324, Westerink.

[13] These real beings are the direct offspring, so to speak, of the Gods – the super-eternal unities which are the productive principles of being – hence Damascius' phrase "dependent of the Gods". See chapter 3 for a fuller explanation of this. It is important to note also, that Damascius, in conformity with the Platonic tradition, describes real beings as being both *living* and *intelligent* – the materialist revision of Platonism over the last few centuries has ignored this very important understanding of the nature of the beings of "the intelligible place."

[14] The contrast between the divine and the human is here seen in terms of integration and disintegration: we can understand this because we are aware that as our thoughts rise upward from material objects to immaterial objects, so our thinking takes on an integrative quality: what seems to be a jumble of unrelated things when viewed through our lower gnostic faculties becomes a meaningful and integrated order once we bring our reason to bear upon them. This is what even the material sciences do, in order to provide an understanding of the world in which we live. The great Orphic myth of the dismemberment of Dionysus was always seen by the Platonists as the archetypal drama of the rational soul's descent into matter. See ch. 4 of my *Seven Myths of the Soul*, The Prometheus Trust, Frome, 2000.

according to the *Timaeus* [42b]; here, however, in combination with 'human' things, he applies the term 'mortal'. Corporeal things have no 'thought', nor even perception, taken by themselves. It is multifarious inasmuch as each part of it is an aggregate of many things and inasmuch as it is divided and material. It is 'dissoluble' because it is composed of many parts; the way in which it is dissolved is the same in which it was composed, either as regards its essence only, or also in time. It is 'never of the same condition and nature', because it is forever changing either in activity or in substance as well.

Let us summarise these two states: In the intelligible place we have real being which is stable and causal, eternal and true. In the material realm we have things which are constantly rising into existence but never really *are*; material things are effects of intelligible causes; they are temporal and in varying degrees deceptive unless their relation to real being, or ideas, is acknowledged. Much of the unspoken "philosophy" of our materialistic civilisation implies that material things are real and abstract things are less real: this is a reversal of the true state of things according to the Platonic tradition. To many modern thinkers abstract things are merely a convenient construct of the mind which imposes a more or less arbitrary order on the mass of real materiality. It is true, of course, that the human mind is creative, and it is this quality which might suggest that the process of abstraction is moving the thinker away from reality; but the first action of the human mind is *discovery*, not *creativity*. Once the mind discovers principles it then naturally starts to use them in the subsequent creative process – but it must be emphasised that we cannot be truly creative unless we have contacted some *already existing* abstraction. Proof of this follows from the fact that if our understanding of the pre-existing principle is too distorted the creative process which follows our flawed discovery will necessarily be limited and carry within it a high degree of destructiveness.

So to return to the Platonic view of reality: We have, up to this point, distinguished between two conditions or worlds – the first is the intelligible world which is the home of real being, the second is the sensible world which is the home of things which are continually rising into, and falling away from, existence. What is the relationship between the two?

At its simplest – and we are here ignoring the different levels of reality within each of the two worlds – we can say that the real being of the intelligible world acts as a *cause* of the material things of the sensible world. To take an example: I want to make a material object which will be useful to a golfer who is lacking a golf ball. I look to the idea of roundness because I will need to make the ball as close to round as possible; I will also need to translate this into a three dimensional roundness – a sphere – rather than a two dimensional circle, so I will also use the idea of three extended dimensions; I will also need to consider size – magnitude – because my planned object must be a certain size in order to be movable by a golf club; I will also consider colour, so that the conventions of golf are observed and so that once the ball is hit into the green fairway it is still visible to the player who may not have seen its exact resting place. There are, of course, other ideas I will have to have thought about – weight, strength, tension, and so on, if I am to make a usable golf ball. Now none of these ideas are in themselves sensible and material: I have never seen the perfect circle with my physical sight, only things which approximate to a perfect circle. Nor have I ever contacted pure strength with any of my senses; only things which in varying degrees are strong. But as a intellectual being I have contact with ideas, and if I understand them properly I will be able to use them as suitable paradigms for making my intended object.

Now according to Plato these intelligible things – ideas – are the paradigms for all material things; each idea being capable of almost unlimited application. However often I want to create a golf ball I only have to contact the same small set of ideas – as Mr Dunlop knows, you can make millions of golf balls from the same model. To go up the scale a little, the idea of roundness not only stands as one of the paradigms for a golf ball, but also for a wheel, a figure in dance, a basis for a dome, a formation of parts of many letters, and so on and on. Over the centuries Platonic philosophers have seen ideas as if they were seals able to make an impression on wax over and over again, as a real thing able to be reflected by any number of mirrors, and as an artist's model able to be portrayed over and over again.

I have given an example in terms of human creativity, where we can best see the use of abstract ideas in the bringing into existence of material things; but Plato uses the same model for the creation of everything – from the smallest thing in the natural universe to the universe itself considered as a whole. This is made clear in the *Timaeus* (29a) in which the Demiurgus (Zeus) – the creator of the whole manifested universe is said to look to a paradigm. Proclus, commenting on this says:[15]

> "If indeed the fabrication of wholes is indefinite and without design, there is not a paradigmatic cause of the universe; but if it is not lawful to conceive this to be the case, and the Demiurgus knows what he produces, and knowing thus produces the fabrication of the world, the causes of the things generated are contained in him, and it is necessary either that he should primarily possess these causes, or that they should be imparted to him by more ancient principles. But whichever of these we admit, there is a paradigmatic cause prior to the world. Farther still, since the Demiurgus is intellect, if he produces by his very being, he produces that which is most similar to himself. But this is to produce an image of himself."

Thus we can see that there is an important similarity between the small acts of creation that we perform, and that which brought the whole universe into being: in both instances the creator holds an intellectual model in abstract. Of course, the human mind is involved in time and therefore process, so that we generally have to pursue ideas before they become actively creative – the same cannot be said for the eternal creator, who, as Proclus points out, "produces by his very being".

Plato uses several examples in his writings of the causal and creative power of ideas (which, of course, many modern scholars call "forms"). Two passages concerning the idea of beauty will, I think suffice: the first is from the *Symposium* (211a) in which Socrates reports the words of Diotima as she described the vision of Beauty itself, the paradigm of all beautiful things:

> "It [Intelligible Beauty] resides not in any other being, not in any animal, for instance; nor in the earth, nor in the heavens, nor in any other part of the universe: but, simple and separate from other things, it subsists alone with itself, and possesses an essence eternally uniform. All other forms which are beauteous participate of this; but in such a manner they participate, that by their generation or destruction this suffers no diminution, receives no addition, nor undergoes any kind of alteration."

In this extract the important principle of the paradigm being exempt from its own effects is shown by the last sentence: no matter how many

---

[15] Commentary on the Timaeus, 98A.

mirrors are set around an object, the fact that it is reflected makes no difference to the object itself. The second extract is from the *Phaedo* (100b ff):

> *Socrates*: However, I now assert nothing new, but what I have always asserted at other times, and in the preceding disputation. For I shall now attempt to demonstrate to you that species of cause which I have been discoursing about, and shall return again to those particulars which are so much celebrated; beginning from these, and laying down as an hypothesis, that there is a certain something beautiful, itself subsisting by itself; and a certain something good and great, and so of all the rest; which if you permit me to do, and allow that such things have a subsistence, I hope that I shall be able from these to demonstrate this cause to you, and discover that the soul is immortal.

> *Cebes*: But, in consequence of having granted you this already, you cannot be hindered from drawing such a conclusion.

> *Socrates*: But consider the things consequent to these, and see whether you will then likewise agree with me. For it appears to me, that if there be any thing else beautiful, besides the beautiful itself, it cannot be beautiful on any other account than because it participates of the beautiful itself; and I should speak in the same manner of all things. Do you admit such a cause?

> *Cebes*: I admit it.

> *Socrates*: I do not therefore any longer perceive, nor am I able to understand, those other *wise* causes;[16] but if any one tells me why a certain thing is beautiful, and assigns as a reason, either its possessing a florid colour, or figure, or something else of this kind, I bid farewell to other hypotheses (for in all others I find myself disturbed); but this I retain with myself, simply, unartificially, and perhaps foolishly, that nothing else causes it to be beautiful, than either the presence, or communion, or in whatever manner the operations may take place, of the beautiful itself. For I cannot yet affirm how this takes place; but only this, that all beautiful things become such through the beautiful itself. For it appears to me

---

[16] Socrates uses the phrase *wise causes* ironically: material and instrumental causes (which he is dismissing here) are, of course, a part of the explanation of things – but without an understanding of more powerful and organising causes which are centred on ideas and purposes, the investigation of the mechanical causes of things is a task belonging to Sisyphus. See chapter 5 and its postscript for a fuller explanation of this.

most safe thus to answer both myself and others; and adhering to this, I think that I can never fall, but that I shall be secure in answering, that all beautiful things are beautiful through the beautiful itself. Does it not also appear so to you?

Cebes: It does.

Over the centuries there have been those who have taken Plato's "theory of Forms" at a superficial level, and declared that the intelligible realm is the only reality and the only good, while the sensible realm is unreal and evil: this is a grave misunderstanding of the doctrine. There is no doubt that Plato claims a greater reality for the higher realm - simply because its inhabitants are causal and permanent, while the lower realm is populated by things which are merely effects and temporal. But the other side of the argument is clear: if real being is good and is causal, its effects, too, must be good - otherwise the good of real being is limited and does not have the power to transmit its essential goodness to its productions. All Plato and his followers insist upon is, firstly, that the value of material things is entirely dependent upon their originating causes; and, secondly, that a rational creature - such as ourselves - must not become so blinded by matter that the intelligible causes of the higher realm are removed from view, for every creature is closest to perfection - and therefore happiest - when active at their most intrinsic level.[17]

Plato's theory of forms thus unfolded is the basis for understanding the ontology and metaphysics of the Platonic tradition; but one final point needs to be considered. This metaphysical doctrine is closely related to that of Plato's epistemology – his doctrine of human knowledge – which, I think, is worth outlining here.

How is it that we can discover truth? If we already know all truth then we do not need to go through the process of discovering it; on the other hand, if we do not know truth how do we recognise it when we come across it in our discovery? Plato answers this problem by suggesting that the human soul has innate within its rational nature all the intellectual principles through which, as we have seen above, the cosmos is created. But this possession of principles is not one which is fully actualised because our intellect is, at least in our ordinary condition, submerged in the process of time – which is antithetical to the nature of true ideas. What this means is that our possession of principles is to a certain degree lost in the forgetfulness of dark matter: true education, then, is the

---

[17] For a more detailed look at this important clarification see my essay 'Diotima's Continuum of Love' in the Prometheus Trust Students' Edition of *The Symposium*.

recovery of forgotten memories. When we perceive an approximate circle in the external world through our senses our mind extracts the idea which subsists as a universal within it and reminds us of the perfect circle which resides in the intelligible place.

This process is laborious: we normally need to approach the universal idea through many different manifestations of it in particular things before we really begin to separate the true principle from the other accidental qualities which adhere to it in its various material expressions. The two doctrines, that of Forms and that of Innate Ideas, support and confirm one another: the reality of the pre-subisting ideas that underlie all things is confirmed by our recognition of them; the qualified possession of ideas by the soul is a natural consequent to the metaphysical view of creation which says that no real thing can exist without the appropriate reception of ideas.

The subject is more fully explored in a companion volume in this series – *The Unfolding Wings* – which deals with the Platonic view of the path to perfection.

Chapter Two

Some Necessary Concepts

The first chapter of this section has outlined what one might call the orthodox view of Plato's Theory of Forms. I have emphasised one aspect which is sometimes neglected, which otherwise would move Plato's teaching into dualism, but with this exception my overview is much the same as is given in many college courses today.

In broad terms, this simple view of Plato's metaphysics has its merits - and certainly in comparison with the inverted model of materialism so widely held in our culture its draws the student towards a clearer view of reality. Nevertheless if we are content with this paradigm as it stands it poses more questions than it answers, and its enemies can easily find apparent flaws. The rest of this section is devoted to widening and deepening this initial view into the true Platonic world view. To develop the outline into a coherent and comprehensive vision of reality we need to follow the thinking of the later Platonists (sometimes inaccurately called the neoplatonists). You will have noticed that the quotes I have used in chapter one are almost entirely drawn from Plato's own writings: from this point on I will draw more heavily upon the later Platonists, and allow Plato's implied teachings to emerge from their writings. Perhaps a small diversion is needed here to justify this dependence upon philosophers who come many centuries after Plato himself.

That the writings of Plato are only an approximate and simplified outline of his full teaching cannot be seriously disputed: In the *Phaedrus* (at 274e ff) Socrates gives an account of the beginnings of writing and the reply that the King of Egypt, Thaumus, gave to Theuth when the latter presented the King with his invention of writing, claiming it to be of great advantage to the human race:

> "O most artificial[18] Theuth, one person is more adapted to
> artificial operations, but another to judging what detriment or
> advantage will arise from the use of these productions of art: and
> now you who are the father of letters, through the benevolence
> of your disposition, have affirmed just the contrary of what

---

[18] The translation is Taylor's, and since his time some words have shifted in meaning: here *artificial* is used to mean that which pertains to art, rather than that which is false.

letters are able to effect. For these, through the negligence of recollection, will produce oblivion in the soul of the learner; because, through trusting to the external and foreign marks of writing, they will not exercise the internal powers of recollection. So that you have not discovered the medicine of memory, but of admonition. You will likewise deliver to your disciples an opinion of wisdom, and not truth. For, in consequence of having many readers without the instruction of a master, the multitude will appear to be knowing in many things of which they are at the same time ignorant; and will become troublesome associates, in consequence of possessing an opinion of wisdom, instead of wisdom itself."

Plato develops this theme and shows how the best teaching is based not on the written word but on the oral tradition which allows the teacher to speak to the soul of the pupil:[19] the written work is unable to distinguish when a truth is to be unfolded and to whom; but the spoken discourse is a living thing which brings about true wisdom. The passage of this dialogue ends with Socrates saying (at 276e ff):

In my opinion, a much more beautiful study will result from discourses, when some one employing the dialectic art, and receiving a soul properly adapted for his purpose, plants and sows in it discourses, in conjunction with science; discourses which are sufficiently able to assist both themselves and their planter, and which are not barren, but abound with seed; from whence others springing up in different manners, are always sufficient to extend this immortal benefit, and to render their possessor blessed in as high a degree as is possible to man.

---

[19] *Phædrus* [275d ff]: "That which is committed to writing contains something very weighty, and truly similar to a picture. For the offspring of a picture project as if they were alive; but, if you ask them any question, they are silent in a perfectly venerable manner. Just so with respect to written discourses, you would think that they spoke as if they possessed some portion of wisdom. But if, desirous to be instructed, you interrogate them about any thing which they assert, they signify one thing only, and this always the same. And every discourse, when it is once written, is every where similarly rolled among its auditors, and even among those by whom it ought not to be heard; and is perfectly ignorant, to whom it is proper to address itself, and to whom not. But when it is faulty or unjustly reviled, it always requires the assistance of its father. For, as to itself, it can neither resist its adversary, nor defend itself.. . . But there is another discourse, and how much better and more powerful it is born than this . . . . that which, in conjunction with science, *is written in the soul of the learner,* which is able to defend itself, and which knows to whom it ought to speak, and before whom it ought to be silent."

Plato also writes about the same subject in his seventh letter (at 344c), in which he says that "Every worthy man will be very far from writing about things truly worthy . . . but the objects of his pursuit are situated in a beautiful region." And if we can ignore what Plato himself says about the value he places on the oral tradition, we can hardly ignore the plain statement of his most famous pupil , Aristotle, who refers to his own and Plato's oral teachings.

All of this should be plain enough – if somewhat inconvenient to the scholar's of our age, who in general would like everything neatly written down and tied up – but it is still a matter of some controversy. There should, of course, be arguments over *what* is left unwritten, but not the fact of it. There are signs of the greater acceptance of the primacy of the oral tradition in ancient times – Pierre Hadot writing in his *Philosophy as a Way of Life* says,[20] "More than other literature, philosophical works are link to oral transmission because *ancient philosophy itself is above all oral in character.* Doubtless there are occasions when someone was converted by reading a book, but one would then hasten to the philosopher to ear him speak, question him, and carry on discussions with him and other disciples in a community that always serves as a place of discussion. In matters of philosophic teaching, writing is only an aid to memory, a last resort that will never replace the living word."

Thomas Taylor discusses the development of the Platonic tradition between the time of Plato and that of the latter Platonists (whose writings start with those of Plotinus in 3rd century CE and end with those of Simplicius whose work continued after the closure of the Athenian Academy in 529 CE) in his fine essay *On the History of the Restoration of the Platonic Theology.*[21] In this he suggests that while the philosophers of early antiquity were content to pass on the inner truths of Pythagoras and Plato from teacher to pupil through the living discourse of the oral tradition, those of later antiquity became more open in their writings because the new dispensation of Christianity, increasing dominant numerically and politically, was hostile to their philosophy. Under these circumstances the fragile construct of the oral tradition became less and less viable and the last few pagan sages – Proclus, Olympiodorus, Damascius and Simplicius – attempted to write what before had only been spoken. The subtleties which are only hinted at in the dialogues of Plato are clearly developed in

---

[20] *Philosophy as a Way of Life*, Pierre Hadot, trans. M Chase, Blackwell, Oxford, 1995, p. 62. The italics are mine.

[21] See volume VII of the Thomas Taylor Series, *Oracles and Mysteries*.

the writings of these philosophers, and for this reason our remaining chapters rely more upon them than upon the works of Plato.

One final point might be made while we consider how this conflict between Christianity and paganism affected our philosophic heritage. Our age tends to separate philosophy and religion – and indeed many other areas of human endeavour – and it would seem from most of the extant texts of antiquity that there was a similar separation in that age: I would claim this to be far from the truth. The error of the orthodox view of ancient philosophy arises partly because of our own culturally limited assumptions about the relationship between philosophy and religion, but mainly because of the distortion caused by the monopoly in learning held by the church in Europe between the closure of the pagan academies in the sixth century CE and the Protestant reformation in northern Europe in the sixteenth century. Over this millennium there was an element of active suppression, but its effect was relatively limited: more importantly the systematic copying of manuscripts remained almost entirely in the hands of the monasteries. Under these circumstances what tended to get selected for copying were those writings which were considered as useful and true – and this did not include overtly pagan texts. Without continuous copying and care writings before the printing revolution would easily be lost; and so it is that the texts we have from the ancient pagan philosophers tend to be those which are more concerned with theoretical philosophy than those of a more devotional nature. For this reason the truth that the doctrine of the Gods is central to the ancient philosophy is largely overlooked, and the wholistic nature of the ancient world-view is obscured.

Having made at least a *prima facie* case for the later Platonists to be seen as the inheritors of the inner Platonic teachings, let us look at some of the basic concepts which will allow us to get a deeper understanding of how the universe unfolds from its divine source.

The concept of participation

We have already seen that mundane things are as they are because they receive characteristic qualities from the eternal ideas or forms of the intelligible realm: in this respect we can say that the material thing *participates* in the form. Thus a human system of justice is just only insofar as it participates in the idea of justice itself, receiving from it the essential characteristics inherent in the idea, and likewise, a thing is a unity only insofar as it participates in unity itself. At its simplest this scheme relies on three distinct things: let us use a simple example.

A sculptor is making a statue of a nymph: he plans to make the nymph beautiful and through a combination of properly exercised imagination and craft he does so. He has looked to the idea of beauty; if he is a truly enlightened human being he will have looked as directly as anyone can upon the beautiful itself, while insofar as he falls short of full enlightenment, so his view will in the same degree be obscured and distorted – but nevertheless he has to a certain extent viewed this eternal idea. We can say that this beauty is *unparticipated beauty*. As the marble (or whatever material is being worked) takes on its beautiful proportions and figure we can say that the beauty held by the statue is *participated beauty*. And we can say that the marble is the *participant*.

What is the difference between unparticipated beauty and participated beauty? Taylor defines the imparticipable as "that which is not consubsistent with a subordinate nature." In our example the participated beauty of the statue only comes into existence with the statue, it will subsist with it for the duration of the existence of the statue, and will cease to exist at the same time as the statue ceases to exist. The unparticipated beauty, on the other hand, pre-existed the statue (for its maker saw the beauty before a chisel was laid upon the marble), its subsistence is not dependent in any way upon the existence of the statue, and it will continue to exist after the marble has crumbled into dust. This important distinction rests upon the fact that while we may separate the participated beauty from its material recipient in our minds for the purposes of analysis, the unparticipated is *actually* separate, and is therefore called by Proclus "the self-sufficient".

Because this distinction is easily blurred by those who have read Plato but not his later commentators, I find it best to refer to the *unparticipable* as the *idea* and the *participable* as the *form* – and in this I am really following Aristotle who writes in his *Metaphysics* (987b) when comparing Plato's teaching to that of the Pythagoreans:

> "Things of this kind, therefore, Plato denominated *ideas* [ιδεας, ideas], but asserted that all sensible things were denominated as different from, and as subsisting according to these. For, according to him, the multitude of things synonymous is homonymous to forms [ςιδος, eidos] according to particpation; but he only changed the name participation."

To summarise, the three terms involved in this relationship are:

The imparticipable – that which is above the participant.
The participable – that which is an inseparable part of the participant.

The participant – that which is receptive of the dynamic power of the imparticipable.

As an aid to further study in various texts this table may be of some use:

Greek	Transliteration	Term	Alternative term
αμεθεκτον	amethekton	unparticipable	unpossessed
μεθεκτον	methekton	participable	possessed
μετεχον	metechon	participant	possessor

We need to look at the salient features of this system of participation and the clearest exposition of them is to be found in Proclus *Elements of Theology*, especially in propositions 23 and 24, the first of which states that "Every imparticipable produces the things which are participated, and all participables are extended to (or strive towards) the imparticipable": in other words the *idea* acts not only as a producing cause to its effects, but also that it acts as a final goal – and lends a kind of continuing creative tension within the various forms of which it was the originator. The second proposition states that "Every thing which participates is inferior to that which is participated; and that which is participated is inferior to that which is imparticipable." So that we have a clear hierarchy which, starting from the bottom, comprises *matter – form – idea*, or *participant – participable – unparticipable*; each term depending on that which is above it for its perfection.

To go back to our example, the marble is perfected by the imposition of a form upon it; and the dynamic nature of the individualised form which the sculptor has united with in the creative process has brought the particular statue of the nymph into existence. But this form has in turn been produced by the much more dynamic qualities of the imparticipated idea of beauty which by its very nature throws off an infinite varities of forms, like sparks from a fire.

We will see in the following chapters how this fundamental threefold pattern is repeated at every level of reality. We will also see how it can be extended through a longer chain of terms by considering a participant at the lower end of one chain to be a unparticipated entity at the head of a lower chain. The first unfolding of this pattern is the universal participation of all things in the characteristics of The One, and I have added as an appendix to this volume the first six propositions of Proclus' *Elements of Theology*, as a masterly exposition of this pattern.

This scheme is the simplest and most elegant by which individual things are truly related to the highest divine causes - as E R Dodds says in his notes on Proclus' proposition 23: "It embodies in its clearest shape the Neoplatonic solution first raised in Plato's *Parmenides*, the problem of reconciling the necessary immanence of the Forms with their necessary transcendence. If participation is to be real, the Form must be immanent, and therefore divided; if it is to be participation of one undivided principle, the Form must be transcendent, and therefore not directly participated. . . . What is directly participated is an immanent universal. . . . . The transcendent universal must exist, in order to give unity to the many immanent universals." We thus come back to the idea that Plato and his true disciples do not see the material world as empty of meaning, or of divinity, but filled with both through the mechanism of this threefold scheme of participation.

Unity, being and knowledge

What is it that we can know? It is quite clear that we can only know things that possess unity and being, and that we cannot know absolute multiplicity and non-being as such. When we want to know some material thing we naturally look for its causes - and especially its formal or essential cause - because it is this rather than its adventitious matter that possesses unity and being. Indeed, as we approach matter which is empty of form - in other words matter with the least degree of unity and being - so our gnostic faculties fail us and we find it impossible to think of it without introducing some kind of phantom characteristic. As Plato says in the *Timaeus* (at 52b) of that which is receptive of form, but *is not* itself:

"This indeed is tangible without tangent perception; and is scarcely by a certain spurious reasoning the object of belief. Besides, when we attempt to behold this nature, we perceive nothing but the delusions of dreams, and assert that every being must necessarily be somewhere, and be situated in a certain place: and we by no means think that any thing can exist, which is neither in the earth nor comprehended by the heavens. All these, and all such opinions as are the sisters of these, we are not able to separate from our cogitation of that which subsists about a vigilant and true nature: and this because we cannot rouse ourselves from this fallacious and dreaming energy, and perceive that in reality it is proper for an image to subsist in something different from itself; since that in which it is generated has no proper resemblance of its own, but perpetually exhibits the phantasm of something else; and can only participate of essence in a certain imperfect degree, or it would become in every respect a perfect non-entity."

In contrast, that which has being is the proper object of our intellect and the higher the degree of unity and being, the better we can know the object. The passage continues:

> "But to true being, true reason bears an assisting testimony, through the accuracy of its decisions; affirming, that as long as two things are different from each other, each can never become so situated in either, as to produce at the same time one thing, and two things essentially the same."

Why is this so important? Because in exploring Platonic metaphysics we must understand that each level of the universe has its appropriate human level of perception: sensible objects are perceived through the senses, while ideas are perceived through the intellect. If we attempt to inspect anything with a faculty which is lower than the thing itself we are really seeing its effects rather than the thing in itself; conversely if we attempt to inspect a thing with a faculty which is active on a higher level than the thing itself, we are contemplating its causes rather than the thing in itself. Neither of these two activities are wrong - but we must be aware that this is what we are doing. Furthermore we should be aware that every human being has a natural gravity when exercising him- or herself gnostically towards reason: as soon as we see a sensible object we begin the process of rational abstraction - in other words we automatically re-interpret the information we receive through our senses and the faculty which unites the senses' perceptions into a whole. This re-interpretation almost effortlessly rearranges the sense perceptions into a series of causal principles. *Likewise the tendency towards the reason moves the imparticipable unities downwards towards participable universals in our minds*: the higher we go in the scheme of things, the more we need to consciously exercise our intuitional and contemplative faculties in order to see the real being or idea, rather than its effects. As Proclus says[22] "The soul through its own mental faculty possesses precise knowledge of real beings. By being established in the intellective level of itself, it understands all with simple and indivisible intuition. Moving towards the One, the soul brings together all the plurality within it, acts with divine enthusiasm and touches that which is above intellect."

The concept of conversion

We have looked at the concept of participation, at least in outline, and discussed it in terms of a downward movement from the highest unities

---

[22] On the Chaldaean Philosophy, 4.1-11.

towards the lowest and most particularised concrete things: we have established, in this way, a mechanism whereby real being acts as a cause to the whole universe. If we stopped here we would have postulated a universe in which real communication was only in one direction - from the top down. In such a universe entropy rules: all true movement is from the better to the worse, from being to non-being, from power to impotence, and the dualistic doctrines which have done so much to undermine our culture would be proved right. But this is not the universe of the Platonic tradition, despite some superficial readings to the contrary.

There is an important threefold "movement" within the metaphysical framework of Platonism which may be described as one of abiding-proceeding-converting; it is sometimes known as the circular path. Proclus deals with this important concept in the 35th proposition of his *Elements of Theology* and its accompanying argument:

> "*Everything caused abides in, proceeds from, and returns to, its cause.* For if it alone abided, it would in no respect differ from its cause, since it would be without separation and distinction from it. For progression is accompanied with separation. But if it alone proceeded, it would be unconjoined and deprived of sympathy with its cause, having no communication with it whatever. And if it were alone converted, how can that which has not its essence from the cause be essentially converted to that which is foreign to its nature? But if it should abide and proceed, but should not return, how will there be a natural desire to everything of well-being and of good, and an excitation to its generating cause? And if it should proceed and return, but should not abide, how, being separated from its cause, will it hasten to be conjoined with it? For it was unconjoined prior to its departure; since, if it had been conjoined, it would entirely have abided in it. But if it should abide and return, but should not proceed, how can that which is not separated be able to revert to its cause? For every thing which is converted resembles that which is resolved into the nature from which it is essentially divided."

We will see in the following chapters how this principle of conversion or return ensures an integrity at every level of the universe, as well as acting as a universal principle which binds the entire universe into a complete and undivided whole.

Essence, power and energy

An important part of the metaphysical analysis of Platonism is the concept of essence-power-energy: what does this mean?

Simply put, in our universe of being we must understand that everything is primarily an essence; from this essence emerges a power; when the power acts it energises.

Let us take an example. Man is in essence a rational being and because of this always has the power to think reasonably; when he is asleep his power of reason is not manifested and so he does not actualise the rational energies and they are said to be "in capacity". But when awake and called upon to think rationally he is not only an essentially rational being with rational powers, but he also actualises his rational energies. We can see that energies are not necessarily present at all times, while essence must always be present (man is always essentially rational, even when circumstances such as disease or sleep prevent the externalisation of this essence); powers hold a middle position in this scheme and from one point of view must always be present in some form, but not necessarily completely so. Our powers of reason are unfolded by their exercise, so that before this the powers are to a certain extent dormant.

One of the basic rules of this analysis is that for every energy there is a power which is adequate to bring the energy into existence, and that for every power there is an essence adequate to bring the power into existence. Thus, to revert to our example, if man is seen to display rational energies we may be certain that he has rational powers; and because of this we may be certain that man's essence is at least at the level of reason, although it may be higher. This rule of adequacy is an absolute: no essence can bring into existence a power greater than itself, nor can any power exercise an energy greater than itself. Thus an animal which is essentially sensitive cannot exercise rational powers because reason is above sense. Nor can a rock, which is essentially mineral, and therefore below the sensitive realm, possess sensitive powers - and still less rational powers - and because it does not possess sensitive powers it cannot actualise sensitive energies.

A being therefore cannot, of itself, act in a realm higher than its own essence. It can act at the level of its essence, or at a lower level. This is important when we come to consider how the universe unfolds itself in such a way as to fill all possible levels of being, activity and consciousness. For example if we see the universe as consisting of three levels - eternal, perpetual and temporal - we can postulate that some beings are eternal in essence, power and energy, while at the other end of the scale there must be beings which are temporal in essence, power and energy. In between there are beings which, for example, are eternal in essence, perpetual in power and temporal in energy.

Triadic concepts

The student may now be starting to see patterns in these preliminary concepts – they all rely strongly upon triplicities. I think it worth looking at these a little more closely, with a view to gathering them together.

In the concept of conversion we have a fundamental triplicity of abiding-proceeding-converting, and in the section on essence, power and energy we can see that essence abides, power proceeds and energy (or activity) converts. Likewise we can see that unity abides, being proceeds and knowledge converts: this last triad is of particular help when reading the *Enneads* of Plotinus because these are firmly based on the doctrine of the "three hypostases" of The One, Intellect and Soul. In the Plotinian system The One acts as the great unmoving centre of reality, true being (intellect) shows forth the hidden depths of The One, and soul seeks to return to The One by converting itself and its works to intellect. Of course we must be careful here, because a common mistake is to reduce The One to a part of a co-equal triad, which is certainly not the truth.

Again, it is reasonably clear that the unparticipable abides in its pure state; the participated universal proceeds as a creative force into informed things; and the participant (or recipient of the characteristic) is converted into a likeness of the original idea or archetype.

These correlated triplicities repeat themselves in many forms throughout the Platonic teachings and were certainly a recognised teaching structure in the Athenian Academy of late antiquity, if not before.

Chapter Three

The Magnificent Repository

". . . . there is not any thing in this universe with which this place is not replete."

Up to this point we have looked at the most hidden truths of reality through the magnificent writings of the Ancients. We have also looked at the orthodox view of modern commentators on Plato's so-called theory of forms. And we have, in the previous chapter, armed ourselves with some useful concepts with which to pursue the greater truths of the Platonic tradition. Our starting point has been the profundity of the doctrine of the One and the Gods: the truths of this golden teaching are discerned with the greatest difficulty because they are so directly rooted in the unknowable One, and the order – or more properly the quasi-order – in which they emerge subsists before the intelligibility of being.

What we turn to now is more easily contemplated by the mind, although in its highest aspects it will still require the eye of the mind to be pure, single-pointed and deeply focused; the great principles of this universe are only to be understood by intuition and reason acting in harmony.

Let us begin this section with a re-statement of one of the fundamental truths of Platonic philosophy: *all things arise with the primary purpose of receiving and further transmitting the Goodness of The One*. Since the transmission of good would fail if a gap were left at any point between The One and the furthest reaches of the universe,[23] we can be sure that every level of the universe is filled with the appropriate conductors of good. Thus we have affirmed that The One is surrounded by Gods who begin to unfold into light the many characteristics which are held in The One in a most occult and unific form. As Thomas Taylor says in his introduction to *The Theology of Plato*:[24]

---

[23] This is similar to the way in which energies such as electricity require the presence of a continuous conductor.

[24] *The Theology of Plato*, Proclus, TTS vol. VIII, p. 2.

The scientific reasoning from which this dogma is deduced is the following: As the principle of all things is *The One,* it is necessary that the progression of beings should be continued, and that no vacuum should intervene either in incorporeal or corporeal natures. It is also necessary that every thing which has a natural progression should proceed through similitude. In consequence of this, it is likewise necessary that every producing principle should generate a number of the same order with itself, *viz. nature,* a natural number; *soul,* one that is psychical (*i.e.* belonging to soul); and *intellect,* an intellectual number. For if whatever possesses a power of generating, generates similars prior to dissimilars, every cause must deliver its own form and characteristic peculiarity to its progeny; and before it generates that which gives subsistence to progressions far distant and separate from its nature, it must constitute things proximate to itself according to essence, and conjoined with it through similitude. It is therefore necessary from these premises, since there is one unity (the principle of the universe), that this unity should produce from itself, prior to every thing else, a multitude of natures characterised by unity, and a number the most of all things allied to its cause; and these natures are no other than the Gods.

We have, then, affirmed that the One produces Gods, not by any process – either temporal or eternal – but by the unenvying power which overflows from the Absolute Good. And since these Gods are most allied to the unity and goodness of the One, they too seek to communicate the providential goodness which is their very quintessence. But if this plurality of Ones is to communicate goodness, what is needed as the next link in the chain?

The answer to this most basic of questions is that there must be real things which can receive the providential energies of the Gods: these real things must be of such an order that they can receive these infinite energies in the most perfect possible way. The primary characteristic of such things must be *being* or *is-ness* – for without being no other characteristic can exist in any way (except, as has been shown, pure unity, which is the state of the Gods). From this point of view the rest of reality below that of the Gods can be described by ontology, or the science of being. And as we explore the science of being, I hope the reader will see how the science of ideas – and therefore the theory of forms – is embraced by ontology. This section is called, therefore, *The*

Universe of Being, and I propose to deal with being as unfolding the various possibilities of is-ness.

Let us first return to what has been said of The One and the Gods, using the profoundly inspired passage from Thomas Taylor's introduction to the *Works of Plato* as a summary of what has been discuued in section one:[25]

> "Here then we see the vast empire of deity, an empire terminated upwards by a principle so ineffable that all language is subverted about it, and downwards by the vast body of the world. Immediately subsisting after this immense unknown we in the next place behold a mighty all-comprehending one, which, as being next to that which is in every respect incomprehensible, possesses much of the ineffable and unknown.
>
> From this principle of principles, in which all things causally subsist absorbed in superessential light and involved in unfathomable depths, we view a beauteous progeny of principles, all largely partaking of the ineffable, all stamped with the occult characters of deity, all possessing an overflowing fullness of good. From these dazzling summits, these ineffable blossoms, these divine propagations, we next see being, life, intellect, soul, nature and body depending; *monads* suspended from *unities*, deified natures proceeding from deities.
>
> Each of these monads too, is the leader of a series which extends from itself to the last of things, and which while it proceeds from, at the same time abides in, and returns to its leader. And all these principles and all their progeny are finally centred and rooted by their summits in the first great all-comprehending one. Thus all beings proceed from, and are comprehended in the first being; all intellects emanate from one first intellect; all souls from one first soul; all natures blossom from one first nature; and all bodies proceed from the vital and luminous body of the world. And lastly, all these great monads are comprehended in the first one, from which both they and all their depending series are unfolded into light. Hence this first one is truly the unity of unities, the monad of monads, the principle of principles, the God of gods, one and all things, and yet one prior to all."

Here again we see that the first of the six monads mentioned is *being*: the other five – life, intellect, soul, nature and body – we will see are re-

---

[25] *The Works of Plato I,* p. 39, TTS vol. IX.

statements of being which reveal the otherwise hidden characteristics of it. We will also see that without *being* the two great connecting powers which fill the universe, causality and intelligibility, would be impossible; for that which *is not* cannot cause other things, nor can that which *is not* be known.

What *being itself* is will become a little clearer if we recall the properties of the super-order from which it arises. Immediately before being are the Unities (or Henads) which, being gathered without media around The One are the 'above-beings' of the ante-cosmos, and it is here in which the two principles of the *Bound* and the *Infinite* remain in their pure and unmingled state. But when these two principles are drawn together they form the first two terms of a most primary triad:

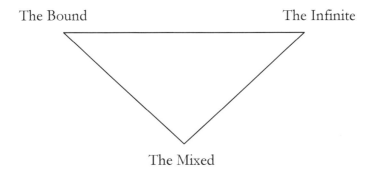

We should be clear at this point that the pure *Bound* and the pure *Infinite* are forever separate,[26] but below this exempt transcendency (their "unparticipated" state) they become participated by the Mixed which we see from these passages from Plato's *Philebus*, is Being:

> *Socrates*: God, we said, has exhibited *the infinite*, and also *the bound* of beings.
>
> *Protagoras*: Very true.
>
> *Socrates*: Let us take these two of the species of things; and for a third let us take that, which is composed of those two mixed together. (23c – d) . . . .

---

[26] As we will see below (page 152), where Damascius in his *Lectures on the Philebus* says, "Limit [or Bound] and Infinitude are twofold: first they appear as principles [*i.e.* causes], then as consequences [*i.e.* effects], for each of the two is present if every existent.

Socrates: But the four sorts having been now described, every one of them distinctly, we should do well, for memory's sake, to enumerate them in order.

Protagoras: No doubt of it.

Socrates: The first then I call infinite; the second bound; the third *essence mixed and generated from these*: and in saying that the cause of this mixture and production is the fourth, should I say aught amiss?

Protagoras: Certainly not. (27b – c)

(The "fourth" mentioned last of all here refers to The One, who produces both the Bound and the Infinite, and causes them to be mixed.)

Thus Plato clearly states that *essence* - in other words, being – is derived from the mixing of bound and infinite and we will see that every re-expression of being, in whatever form this takes, always displays the characteristics which it receives from these great principles. Furthermore the triadic nature of being (bound-infinite-mixed) will also be carried down through its various manifestations and give it its essential intelligibility.

Using our normal triadic diagram we can realign our first diagram to show how the relationship of these three principles is best considered:

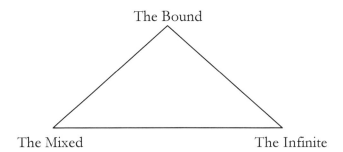

The Bound *abides*: it is most similar to The One, and acts as the essence of essence; the Infinite *proceeds* and acts as the power of essence; the Mixed *converts* and is the activity of essence.

The student who is coming across these ideas for the first time will, perhaps, at this point feel that he or she is unable to comprehend them: my advice is to press on, because as we unpack the idea of being and its order, together with the other five monads and their orders, these fundamental ideas will, I hope, become clearer.

Being, causality and the six orders

We are looking at the universe in this section as the universe of being – why? After the super-existence of The One, and its[27] immediate offspring, the Gods, and their unenvying providence it is necessary that this providential goodness is passed on to some *thing*. But to be a *thing* implies not only unity of some kind but also some is-ness or being. The Gods, therefore, produce *being* so that they may imitate The One, who has produced them: it is only with the production of being that providential powers can become manifest.

With the production of being certain two important characteristics are born: firstly that of *causality*, and secondly that of *intelligibility*. We will return to intelligibility later, but causality at its simplest can be stated in this manner:

Things exist.

Things have the power to produce effects.

Effects exist.

In other words, causality is a single principle which has three fundamental components – *cause, causation*, and *effect*. That which has being can act as a cause, but that which has no being cannot act as a cause: this is a universal truth which admits of no real exceptions. The case of an imagined ill bringing about an actual effect tests this law, but on closer examination it will be seen that the creative power of the human who imagines the ill is lending to it a certain kind of being, and its power to produce an effect will cease when the human ceases to give it its pseudo existence. The important concept here is that this causal chain allows one thing to "become" another: in other words, without the principle of causality the first of principles – The One – would necessarily stay as the *only one*, and that nothing else would have any kind of existence. We must be careful about how we think about the idea of one thing "becoming" another: the principle of the unparticipable means that one thing "becomes" another, while remaining exempt from its creation, and so remains as itself.

Starting with being, as the first of the things which are suspended from unities, we should understand that within being itself are all the other things which are possible in the ontological universe: this is

---

[27] The English language fails here: it cannot provide an appropriate pronoun for The One, who is above duality, so that *He* and *She* should be excluded; and The One is certainly not below the level of duality – which makes the neuter *It* inappropriate. We must get used to the failure of language, when thinking about the highest levels of reality.

certain because, as we have seen, no power or energy can be greater than its abiding essence. Being, as the first ontological term of the universe stands as the abiding essence to all things.

Again, since the unfoldment of the universe is through the principle of similarity, we can say that *pure being* is most like its generator – of all things that *are* it is closest to the Gods in character. Pure being, therefore, most closely resembles the Gods' causal nature, and is the most unific, providential, and least separated of ontological things.

As being itself is most causal, it must have the greatest causative power: this dymanic power is termed *life* – which is the very principle of proceeding power. Life, for this reason constitutes the second term of the ontological universe.

What of the convertive principle, which will give us the first great threefold pattern of abiding-proceeding-converting in the ontological universe? We have already seen, in chapter two, that to the Platonists *being* is the intelligible: what *is*, can be known; what *is not* cannot be known. What converts itself back to the intelligible is *intellect*. This is the third term of the ontological universe: intellect represents the energy or activity of being.

It is this convertive tendency of intellect which we experience as rational beings, and gives to us an important mystical law: *the thinker becomes like the object of his thought.*

We must remember, however, that first triplicity is unific and eternal: therefore the triad is hardly separated at all. Each of these three great principles of the ontological universe are held within the world of pure being as causal entities profoundly united.

Pure being has its own characteristic, and therefore acts in a certain characteristic way: all things which participate of being, therefore, in some sense follow this characteristic. From this it follows that we can talk of an *order of being*, which extends from the highest point of pure being (its *hyparxis*, to use a technical term) to the things which are the most distant image of being. From this point of view, we can say that the universe comprises:

A God of being – a unity above being but which has suspended from this God a deified monad.

A monad of being – a first being, which begins the series of beings. If you read again the quote from Thomas Taylor on page 120 you will see this monad referred to as one of those "deified natures proceeding from deities."

A multiplicity of beings – some closer and some more distant from the monad.

The order of being is one of immutable and causal essence: being as being is entirely intelligible and by no means perceptible to the senses or any faculty which requires figure and form. As one of the three great orders which constitute what one might call the *hyper-cosmos*[28] it is eternal; and as the first of these three orders it is closest to the One – the Gods of this order being those who surround the adytum[29] of the First God. The Gods who rule this order of being are usually referred to as the Intelligible Gods – each of these endowing being with an essential characteristic implied by its primary characteristic.

It is a metaphysical axiom that the higher the cause the greater the number of effects, as Proclus says:[30]

> *Every cause energises prior to the thing caused, and constitutes more effects posterior to it.* For so far as it is *cause* it is more perfect and more powerful than that which is posterior to it, and by reason of this is the cause of more effects. For it is the province of a greater power to produce more, of an equal power to produce equal, and of a less power to produce a less, number of effects . . . if, therefore, the cause is more powerful, it is productive of more numerous effects.

Being, therefore, as the highest thing in the ontological universe is productive of the greatest number of effects: from this point of view we can say that the full order of being stretches not only throughout the intelligible realm, but also throughout the sensible realm, and that even the least existent thing – the subatomic particle which moves into and out of existence in minute fractions of a second – carries with it some characteristic inherited from the monad of being. At the hyparxis of the ontological universe, the first being admits of no non-being, since it is pure being; but as we descend the scale of things which participate of being, so the element of non-being enters as a increasingly dominant characteristic. Entities at the lowest end[31] of the order of being must subsume their element of being into a greater being in order to

---

[28] I call it the hyper-cosmos, because the word cosmos is usually used to describe the created or manifested universe: what we have here is a complete order which is above the created universe.

[29] Adytum – the inner sanctum of a temple (pl. *adyta*).

[30] *Elements of Theology*, proposition and argument 57.

[31] If you are reading Taylor, you will find that he uses the word extremity to mean lowest aspect of any order.

continue in existence: it is this building up of communities of being which allow the extremities of the universal order of being to be converted back to the first being. And, of course, the organisation of these 'communities of being' is the work of intellect in its creative aspect. We have seen that within the order of being there is the principle of life, or the dynamic and proceeding power of being; in the order of being, life retains the primary characteristics of being – which are abiding. In order to move outwards in true procession this abiding principle must create its own proceeding order: this, then, is the second great order of the ontological universe.

The order of *life* represents the processive power of the intelligible realm: again we must have God (or perhaps more properly a Goddess) of Life and a monad of life, from which the series of lives proceed. Like the first order, this order is of an intelligible nature, and its life is eternal. It stands as the middle of the three great hyper-cosmic orders and is known as the intelligible-intellectual order; its Gods are the intelligible-intellectual Gods. The real beings of the first order can be seen as primarily causal: the living beings of this second order can be seen as primarily ideas, for it is here that the infinitely powerful ideas or archetypes of deity beam their immortal light like rays leaping from the sun across the universe.[32] The God who is said to rule the lowest extremity of the Intelligible realm is said to be *Phanes* ("light" or "showing forth"): standing, therefore, immediately above the intelligible-intellectual realm his light is taken up as the leading characteristic of this order. As Proclus writes:[33]

> Idea, therefore, truly so called, is an incorporeal cause, exempt from its participants, is an immovable essence, is a paradigm only and truly, and is intelligible to souls from images, but has a causal knowledge of things which subsist according to it. So that from all the doubts we derive one definition of idea truly so called. Hence, those that oppose the doctrine of ideas, should oppose this definition, and not assuming corporeal imaginations of them, or considering them as coarranged with sensibles, or an unessential,

---

[32] Proclus, in the *Theology of Plato* (TTS vol. VIII, p. 171-172) quotes the Chaldæan oracles concerning this extremity: "Thence a fiery whirlwind sweeping along, obscures the flower of fire, leaping, as the same time, into the cavities of the worlds. For all things thence begin to extend their admirable rays downwards."

[33] Commentary on the Parmenides, 935. See p. 148, *Works of Plato III*, TTS vol. XI. You will see from this note that Proclus defines idea as the imparticipable, rather than the participable; and also that he is clear that ideas are very far from human concepts.

or as coordinate with our knowledge, sophistically discourse concerning them. Let it also be observed that Parmenides says that ideas are Gods, and that they have their subsistence in deity; in the same manner as the Chaldæan oracle also calls them the conceptions of the father: for whatever subsists in deity is a God.

Again we can see within this order – as in the order of being – that its effects are extended onwards into the realms of time: in this case, because the order of life is itself an effect of the order of being, the effects are not quite so universal; in the lower realms all things participate in being, but not all things participate in life.

The last of the three hyper-cosmic orders is that of intellect, which is ruled by the Intellectual Gods: it holds in common with the first two the basic characteristics of the intelligible realm, so that all things in the intellectual order are immutable and eternal, but adds its own characteristic of conversion to complete the first full expression of the abiding-proceeding-converting pattern.

We might remember here that we have seen that being arises because the two great principles after The One, the Bound and the Infinite are mixed. In the first order of being the Bound dominates and particularly endows being with stability; in the second order of life, the Infinite dominates and endows things with dynamic power; but in this third order of intellect, the Mixed itself as a third principle dominates, so that intellect can be seen as the relating of being and life (or the bound in essence and the infinite in life) – so that intellect is always characterised by a threefold relation. From one point of view, although ideas as the light of real beings arise in the second order, it is not until this light has passed through the third order – with its characteristic action – that we have ideas in their complete and useful form.

Thus we can see that this intellectual order represents the activity of the intelligible realm: like life, intellect is first found in the order of being, but just as life creates its own second order to bring about procession away from the abiding, so intellect creates a third order so that what has proceeded can be returned. The object of intellect is the intelligible: but the effect of intellect uniting with its object is creative. In fact all real thought is creative: it may seem that to create things we must act, but in truth action only arises after thought of some kind. Artists often talk of being possessed by an idea which leaves them with no choice but to produce their work of art. So it is, on a much greater scale, with divine intellect: in the unific contemplation of the intelligible paradigm the divine intellect recreates the paradigm in terms of intellect. Before we move on to consider what this new creation is, we should understand that the same considerations apply to the effects of the intellectual order: they extend outwards into further realms, but as this order is the third after being and life, its effects are not so universal as that of life, in just the same way that those of life were not so universal as those of being: thus in this material world all things participate in being, fewer in life, and still fewer in intellect.

The creative act which follows from the union of the creator intellect with ideas proceeding from the first and second orders is described in these inspired words by the Chaldæan oracles:[34]

> The intellect of the Father made a crashing noise,[a] understanding, with unwearied counsel, omniform ideas. But with winged speed they leaped forth from one fountain: for both the counsel and the end were from the Father. In consequence too of being allotted an intellectual fire, they are divided into other intellectual forms: for the king previously placed in the multiform world, an intellectual incorruptible impression, the vestige of which hastening through the world, causes the world to appear invested with form, and replete with all-various ideas, of which there is one fountain. From this fountain other immense distributed ideas rush with a crashing noise, bursting forth about the bodies of the world, and are bourne along its terrible bosoms, like swarms of bees. They turn themselves too on all sides, and nearly in all directions. They are intellectual conceptions from the paternal fountain, plucking abundantly the flower of the fire of sleepless time. But a self-perfect fountain pours forth primogenial ideas from the primary vigour of the Father.

We can see, then, that the result of conversion by intellect is the creation of a "projected" universe in which the paradigm of the eternal is repeated in terms of time. For the fullness of eternity to be expressed in the confines of time the Demiurge (or Second Creator, as he is sometimes called because he creates a second great threefold order, based on the first) must use two strategies: *perpetuity* in which time moves but does not end, and further down the orders, the *replacement of opposites* – or the generation of life from death and death from life. To summarise what we have looked at so far we can draw the following diagram to show the relationship of being, life and intellect:

---

[34] See *Oracles and Mysteries*, p. 34, TTS vol. VII, fragment 37 (Majercik).

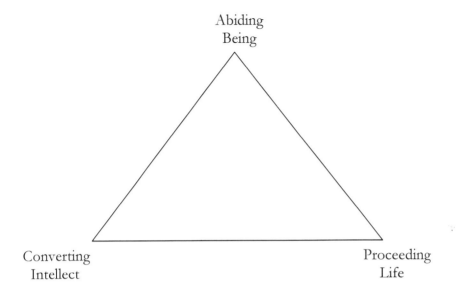

With all production, as we have said before, the immediate effect is most similar to the cause, while that last effect is least like the cause. So it is with the creation of the Demiurge, the divine creative mind. The first order of the so-called second creation is the most intellectual: it is the *order of soul*. But this is intellect reflected in the world of time, therefore the timelessness of the contemplative intellect is transferred into the measured activity of creatures which participate in intellect but are not themselves intellect. The characteristic of the intellectual order is *creativity*, but the characteristic of the order of soul is *moction*. As in every order there is the triad of deity-monad-series, and in the series there are those which are highest in the order which are most like the producing cause, and those which verge to the extremity which are least like the producing cause. In the order of soul there are those that by habitude (or continuous activity) are like intellects, and those that only participate indirectly of intellect. Human souls, according to the ancients, hold a middle place in the order of soul and therefore tend to the middle form of intellectual activity – above sense perception but below pure intuition – which is dianoetic thought. Dianoetic activity, however, always tends to immutable ideas – those eternal sources of reasons – and thus hidden in the human soul is the order of intellect in motion.

Presiding over the order of soul are the Ruling or Super-mundane Gods; these Gods are very close to the Intellectual Gods. As Proclus says:[35]

> For this order is woven together in continuity with the [intellectual] demiurgus and father of wholes, proceeds from, is perfected by, and converted to him, according to his perfective power. Hence also, it is necessary to connect the narration about the governors of the universe, with the discussion concerning the demiurgus, and to assimilate words to the things of which they are the interpreters. For all the series of the ruling Gods, are collected into the intellectual fabrication as into a summit, and subsist about it. And as all the [intelligible-intellectual] fountains are the progeny of the intelligible father, and are filled from him with intelligible union, thus likewise, all the orders of the principles or rulers, are suspended according to nature from the demiurgus, and participate from thence of an intellectual life.

In other words, just as the intelligible-intellectual Gods are gathered around Phanes who rules the extremity of the intelligible order of being producing the light of eternity, so these ruling Gods are gathered around the Demiurge who produces the cosmic triad of orders.

What part does this order play in the scheme of things? While intellect looks to the intelligible and creates the lower world by pure thought,[36] soul looks to the lower world and discovers the intelligible. Soul and intellect constitute the two middle orders of the universe, and as such work closely together in order to co-ordinate the universe as one whole. This is what Proclus says of the Ruling Gods, who are the leaders of all souls and lend to them their distinctive characteristics:

> The assimilative rulers also convert all things to their principles; for every conversion is through similitude. They likewise bind co-ordinate natures to each other. For the communion of the one cause [of all] produces similitude indeed in its participants, but from this, it inserts in them an indissoluble connexion. They also cause all things to sympathize, be friendly, and familiar with each other; exhibiting indeed, through participation, more elevated in more abject natures; but subordinate in more perfect essences, through causal comprehension. They likewise extend series and

---

[35] *The Theology of Plato*, VI, 1, TTS vol. VIII.
[36] Every intellect constitutes the things posterior to itself by thinking, and its creation is in its thinking, and its thought in creating. Proclus, *Elements of Theology*, prop. 174.

periods from on high, as far as to the last of things . . . but collect multitudes into union, through communion according to essence. They also adapt wholes to parts; but comprehend parts in wholes.

In summary we can say that souls, following the pattern of their Gods, regulate, assimilate and co-ordinate. In one way the order particularly reflects the intellectual order, being its immediate offspring; in another way it reproduces the intelligible order, standing in the same position in the cosmic triad of orders as the intelligible in the hyper-cosmic orders. It stands between the eternal intelligible orders which move things but do not themselves move, and the temporal projected orders which are moved. To do this the order of soul is at heart a order of perpetual creatures, who are self-moved. It is this last characteristic, self-movement, which enables the soul to form its true relation to the order of life, and in the same way that the latter order gives life to the whole of the universe, so the soul is especially the life-giver to bodies.

From the abiding order of soul which of course includes human souls – but is not made up exclusively of such – comes the great proceeding order of the manifested universe: that of Nature. The striking fecundity and power of nature is a reflection of the second hyper-cosmic order (of life) which itself is the fountain of dynamic ideas and their overwhelming life-giving power. The powers of nature are not material in themselves, but inextricably linked to matter: this is one of the main differences between the order of soul and the order of nature. The order of soul provides the intelligence which nature, otherwise blind, requires for the proper ordering of matter.

The order of nature draws things through the cycles of time: every action in nature brings a reaction in due time. For this reason the order is sometimes called 'fatal' in the proper sense of the word, meaning that purely natural events and forces bring a never-ending series of things rising into and going out of existence. One of the tasks of the human soul is to come to terms with nature without being entirely overwhelmed by its downward tending energy: as the Chaldæan Oracles say,[37] "You should not look upon Nature, for her name is fatal."

The Gods which rule this order are called liberated, perhaps because the forces they rule over while linked to matter, are not tied to particular forms of matter and are as restless as the ocean, with its ever-changing tides and waves. One might say that the leading characteristic of the order of nature is desire, and the whole of nature is a never-

---

[37] Frag. 70 (Majercik) TTS vol. VII, p. 36.

ending pursuit of goals which are replaced as quickly as they are achieved.

The final order of the cosmic triad is mundane: it is here that the restless energies of nature are shaped by the intellect of soul. It is a convertive order because by the working out of causes of each of the preceding five orders the mundane is a final reflection of the divine source of the universe: Plato called time a flowing image of eternity, and we might say that the mundane order is a flowing image of the intelligible. The Gods which rule this last order are called the Mundane Gods.

In the same way as we laid out the three hypercosmic orders, we can look at the cosmic orders:

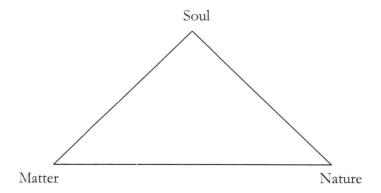

You will notice that in the passage from Taylor's introduction from the Works of Plato, quoted at the beginning of the chapter, the sixth and final monad is called body, rather than matter and we should be clear that the difference between matter and body is important. Body, like the things of the mundane order, is informed (in other words has received forms) since no mundane thing is purely matter. Being, as the first order, *holds all forms as causes*: body, as the ultimate reflection of the first order, *receives all forms as effects*. Proclus, in this treatise on the Subsistence of Evil,[38] shows how pure matter is below the scope of order (its only quality being complete passivity, and able to pass on no quality to anything else in any way). Pure matter is the ultimate reflection of the One, and since the One is not part of any ordered series, neither can we call matter a part of any series.

---

[38] *Essay and Fragments of Proclus*, TTS vol. XVIII.

Summary

The Platonic view of the ontological universe starts with the most abstract and simple thing possible – being. Everything else is a series of re-presentations of *being* clothed in more and more layers of complexity; at each new level of being the causative power is diminished and the intrinsic intelligibility becomes more and more obscured. It is useful to consider the whole as a pyramid of being, with descending layers becoming increasingly darker to the mind. At the summit of this pyramid is pure being: as the descent through the orders continues so the element of non-being becomes ever greater, until at the base of the pyramid the non-entity of matter is touched.

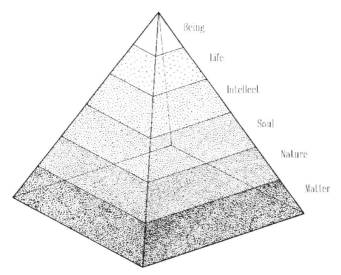

Nevertheless, the unfolded universe is mystically returned to its source by anagogic power, by which its least creature is linked to the highest divinity. There is, to the Platonist, no part of the universe which is not invested with the light of the Gods, and all things are turned to the Good by this light. To summarise these orders we can quote Proclus' *Commentary on the Parmenides* who sees them it terms of processions of Gods who, he says: "may be comprehended in six orders -

The Intelligible,
The Intelligible-Intellectual,
The Intellectual,
The Supermundane,
The Liberated and
The Mundane.

For the *intelligible*, as we have already observed, must hold the first rank, and must consist of *being, life,* and *intellect, i.e.* must *abide, proceed* and *return*, and this super-essentially; at the same time that it is characterized, or subsists principally according to *being*. But, in the next place, that which is both *intelligible* and *intellectual* succeeds, which must likewise be triple, but must principally subsist according to *life,* or *intelligence.* And, in the third place, the *intellectual* order must succeed, which is *triply convertive.* But as, in consequence of the existence of the sensible world, it is necessary that there should be some demiurgic cause of its existence, this cause can only be found in *intellect,* and in the last hypostasis of the *intellectual triad.* For all forms in this hypostasis subsist according to all-various and perfect divisions; and forms can only fabricate when they have a perfect intellectual separation from each other. But since *fabrication* is nothing more than *procession*, the demiurgus will be to the posterior order of the Gods what *The One* is to the orders prior to the *demiurgus*; and consequently he will be that secondarily which the first cause is primarily. Hence, his first production will be an order of Gods analogous to the *intelligible* order, and which is denominated *supermundane.* After this he must produce an order of Gods similar to the *intelligible-intellectual* order, and which are denominated *liberated* Gods. And in the last place, a procession correspondent to the *intellectual* order, and which can be no other than the *mundane* Gods. For the demiurgus is chiefly characterized according to diversity, and is allotted the boundary of all universal hypostases."

I think that one further diagram might illustrate how the orders fit together, how each order provides to the succeeding one an imparticipable characteristic and to its own level a participable characteristic. This diagram is from a D E Wagenhals, who was in communication with Thomas M Johnson in the early years of the twentieth century: it was, says Johnson, one of a number designed as an aid to understanding Proclus' *Theological Elements.* Apart from this diagram and one other added to Johnson's edition of the Elements, the diagrams are now lost. Wagenhals has illustrated proposition 97, which states:

Every archical cause in each series or causal chain imparts to the whole series its characteristic; and that which the cause is primarily, the series is according to diminution.

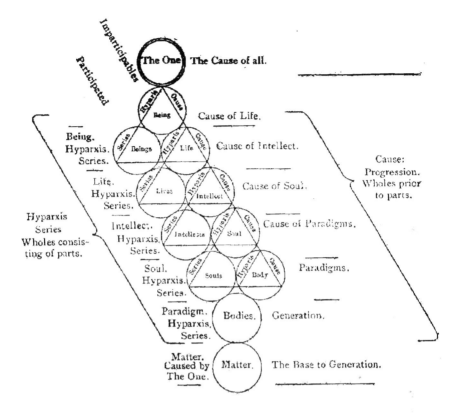

The diagram does not place nature between soul and body – nature as a separate order was sometimes ignored and included in the idea of body – but nevertheless, with the repeating pattern of the diagram, the reader will no doubt be able to imagine how this order would fit in the given scheme.

Now we have explored the deep levels of Platonic metaphysics we might well return to Socrates description of the Cave, with which we started this section: with what we know about the six orders, I am sure the student will begin to notice the accurate description of the cave and the world outside.

Starting at the lowest level, the shadows on the cave wall have the least reality - they are as close to nothingnesses as it is possible for discernable things to be: we will see as we rise with our prisoner how these shadows are the final result of a series of different levels of reality. While the prisoners look at the wall with its dancing shadows they are almost entirely ignorant, and are not able to see themselves, so that the terrible ignorance which is self-ignorance is their lot: this is the state of each of us when our perception is only of materiality. The description of shadows and echoes is one which resembles the mundane order – and the prisoners' lot is that of any human being who believes that the mundane is the only condition of existence.

Now when the prisoner first turns around he sees the statues, furniture and other objects which are being carried along the walled path: these are the representations of higher things. The forms in nature, which continually give rise to actual physical lives and things, are distant echoes of the true ideas of the second order (that of Life). They are in continual movement and still have a high degree of illusiveness about them - Plato says this walled path is like that which "screens the stage of mountebanks on which they exhibit their wonderful tricks."

Beyond the procession of objects is the fire which allows the cave to be a habitable place - a place with a degree of reality and light: the cave without fire would be in utter darkness, and any procession would go undetected. The fire represents the order of soul - each soul being a microcosm of the great sun which the prisoner has not yet glimpsed. The *Timæus* explicitly says that the purpose of souls is to vivify and order the manifested cosmos, which was so often symbolised by the ancients as a cave. The three cosmic orders, then, are represented by the *fire* (soul), the *artificial objects* which are moved along the road (nature) and the *shadows* on the wall (mundane).

Now when our former prisoner has been led to the upper world (from the cosmic orders into the hyper-cosmic orders) Socrates says "And, first of all, he would most easily perceive shadows, afterwards the images of men and of other things in water, and after that the things themselves." The prisoner, then, is at first obliged to look at shadows again - but this time they are shadows of real things, rather than artificial copies. The third (intellectual) order is a perfect reproduction of the two higher orders and the three great intellective gods of the Greek Pantheon - Cronos, Rhea and Zeus - are, respectively Intellective Being, Intellective Life, and Intellect itself. Our introduction into the hyper-cosmic order is through the *order of intellect*, for unless intellect has re-arranged the infinite ideas of the second order into intellectual productions, the dazzling power of pure ideas would be beyond the ability of a mortal to look upon.

The next step is to look at the images of real things reflected in water: the primary ideas of the second *order of life* are the images of the unconditioned beings of the first order. Socrates uses the theme of water here, I think, to indicate the living quality of this vision, for water is the great life-giving element.

Finally the prisoner is able to see the "things themselves" - in other words the authentic and unconditioned eternal beings of the first order. This is the view of the intelligible which is presented to the mind when it has penetrated the veils of every layer of reality which is wrapped about being itself.

This might be the end of the increasing brilliant vision of the former prisoner, but Socrates adds to his joys the contemplation of the heavens: first the lesser lights of the night, and finally the vision of the day-star which the prisoner, now enlightened in every sense, understands as the cause of all things. This is the vision of the Gods, and the One, to which all things return at the end of their journey through the orders of existence and being: the convertive power triumphant – the alone returning to the alone. It is to this final state to which Proclus refers in this most mystical and inspiring passage from his *Theology of Plato* (II, 11):

Let us now therefore, if ever, abandon multiform knowledge, exterminate from ourselves all the variety of life, and in perfect quiet approach near to the cause of all things. For this purpose, let not only opinion and phantasy be at rest, nor the passions alone which impede our anagogic impulse to the first, be at peace; but let the air be still, and the universe itself be still. And let all things extend us with a tranquil power to communion with the ineffable. Let us also, standing there, having transcended the intelligible (if we contain any thing of this kind,) and with nearly closed eyes adoring as it were the rising sun, since it is not lawful for any being whatever intently to behold him - let us survey the sun whence the light of the intelligible Gods proceeds, emerging, as the poets say, from the bosom of the ocean . . . . . And let us as it were celebrate him, not as establishing the earth and the heavens, nor as giving subsistence to souls, and the generations of all animals; for he produced these indeed, but among the last of things; but, prior to these, let us celebrate him as unfolding into light the whole intelligible and intellectual genus of Gods, together with all the supermundane and mundane divinities - as the God of all Gods, the unity of all unities, and beyond the first adyta, - as more ineffable than all silence, and more unknown than all essence, - as holy among the holies, and concealed in the intelligible Gods.

Chapter Four

The Sacred Tetractys

The Pythagoreans held the Tetractys in the highest honour as a sacred key to the truths upon which their system of soul-culture depended. The tetractys is a diagram in triangular form in which four lines of points are arranged: on the highest line there is a single point, below are two points, below this are three points, and the lowest line is made up of four points. There are numerous interpretations and applications of this pattern, but I present one here with a view to giving an overview to the metaphysics of the Platonic tradition, to which Pythagoras himself contributed in no small way.

$$\bullet$$
$$\bullet \qquad \bullet$$
$$\bullet \qquad \bullet \qquad \bullet$$
$$\bullet \qquad \bullet \qquad \bullet \qquad \bullet$$

The highest point - the apex of the triangle - is a representation of *The One*, who is the unity set above all things. *The One* as absolutely transcendent is in no order, although it is possible to think of a kind of order which embraces all things and all possibilities, and which emanates from The One as source and goal. The best term to use for this is the Absolute order. It was held by the Platonists of old that it was impossible to say anything accurately of The One because every quality implies its opposite. Thus if we say that The One is *great* we deny of it the *small*; or if we say of it *he* we deny of it *she*. Any quality added to The One is a diminishing of oneness – it is from this realisation that what is called negative theology arises. Proclus stretches the power of language to its limit in trying to convey to us what is required of us in our approach to *The One*.[39]

It appears, then, that this can only be effected by energizing logically, intellectually, and at the same time divinely, that we may be able to apprehend the demonstrative power of Parmenides, may follow his intuitive perceptions which adhere to true beings, and may in a divinely inspired manner recur to the ineffable and uncircumscribed cosensation of *The One*. For we contain the images of first causes, and participate of total soul, the intellectual extent, and of divine unity. It is requisite, therefore, that we should excite the powers of these which we contain, to the apprehension of the things proposed. Or how can we become near to *The One*, unless by exciting *the one* of our soul, which is as it were an image of the ineffable one? And how can we cause this one and flower of the soul to diffuse its light, unless we first energize according to intellect? For intellectual energy leads the soul to the tranquil energy according to *the one* which we contain. And how can we perfectly obtain intellectual energy, unless we proceed through logical conceptions, and prior to more simple intellections, employ such as are more composite?

Demonstrative power, therefore, is requisite in the assumptions; but intellectual energy in the investigations of beings; (for the orders of being are denied of *The One*) and a divinely-inspired impulse in the cosensation of that which is exempt from all beings, that we may not unconsciously, through an indefinite phantasy, be led from negations to non-being, and its dark immensity. Let us, therefore, by exciting *the one* which we contain, and through this, causing the soul to revive, conjoin ourselves with *The One Itself*, and establish ourselves in it as in a port, standing above every thing intelligible in our nature, and dismissing every other energy, that we may associate with it alone, and may, as it were, dance round it, abandoning those intellections of the soul which are employed about secondary concerns.

We cannot, therefore, in a becoming manner employ affirmations in speaking of this cause, but rather negations of secondary natures; for affirmations hasten to know something of one thing

---

[39] Commentary on the Parmenides, 1072 and 1073-1074, p. 186-7, Works of Plato III, TTS vol. XI.

as present with another. But that which is first is unknown by the knowledge which is connate with beings, and nothing can be admitted as belonging to, or present with, it, but rather as not present: for it is exempt from all composition and participation. To which we may add, that affirmations manifest something definite; for non-man is more infinite than man.

The incomprehensible and uncircumscribed nature of *The One* is therefore more adapted to be manifested through negations: for affirmations may be said to vanquish beings, but negations possess a power of expanding from things circumscribed to the uncircumscribed, and from things distributed in proper boundaries to the indefinite. Can it, therefore, be said that negations are not more adapted to the contemplation of *The One*? For its ineffable, incomprehensible, and unknown nature can alone through these be declared, if it be lawful so to speak, to partial intellectual conceptions such as ours.

Negations, therefore, are better than affirmations, and are adapted to such as are ascending from the partial to the total, from the coordinated to the uncoordinated, and from the circumscribed and vanquished form of knowledge to the uncircumscribed, single, and simple form of energy.

The two points of the second level are the indefinite duad of the Pythagorean system, named the *Bound* and the *Infinite* by Plato, and called *Chaos* and *Ether* by the Chaldeans, which because of its indefinite nature is beyond all science, thought and opinion. The two principles represent an unrelated duality - an absolute positive and an absolute negative, without a connecting body. Again we can only use such phrases as "the great void" or "the empty plenum" to describe this level of reality. It represents the realm of the Gods as Gods, rather than Gods as rulers. Damascius speaks of this in his *Commentary on the Philebus*:[40]

What are the Two Principles and what is the One Principle before them? We hold that the latter is the absolute cause of undifferentiated and unqualified existence, whereas the other two are the causes of existents contradistinguished by certain differences. The primal contra-distinction is that between the unitary and the pluralized, the principles and causes of which have been indicated in different ways by different thinkers; there can be no adequate names for them, since adequate conceptions also are

[40] At 98-102, trans. Westerink, The Prometheus Trust, Westbury, 2011.

lacking; but some call them Limit and Infinitude, others One and Many, others have used whatever terms they thought most fit to indicate them.

Limit and Infinitude are twofold: first they appear as principles [*i.e.* causes], then as consequences [*i.e.* effects], for each of the two is present if every existent.

Not only existents, but *even the Gods originate in Limit and Infinitude*: thus we have male and female, emanative and integrative deities. This does not mean that male deities should not also participate of infinitude, but that limit is the dominating factor, and so on. For being first principles they pervade all things, not some things to the exclusion of others, which would be impossible.

The dyad cannot be primary, for it needs an integrating cause itself, otherwise there would be no coherence in the universe.

The question is how plurality has proceeded from unity. He [Socrates] answers that the first stage is not plurality, but duality, which is next to unity. For it is unthinkable that the manifold should emerge without any middle term immediately after the one, but procession must of necessity be gradual, what is nearer the unit coming first, and so on.[41]

Below the two points are placed the line of three: here we enter the world of the intelligible orders - being, life, intellect – this line, then, represents the hyper-cosmos. Whereas the first two lines (of the one and the duad) are in themselves beyond ordinary knowing, the hyper-cosmos, based as it is on the triad, is most open to the intellect. Every thought we have is based upon the pattern of three, and we extend our knowledge by thinking of one thing and another and their relation. For example we can think of life, the material of a body, and conclude that there is a real thing which has animated the material. We can see this pattern in the simplest syllogistic logic with is major premise, its minor

---

[41] It should be noted regarding this last point that the Greeks did not consider two to be plural: their grammar consisted of singular, dual and plural – in English we have a remnant of this in the use of such words as 'both' which can only be applied to a duad. It was explained mathematically by the fact that a true multiple will produce more when multiplied rather than added (e.g. 3x3 = 9, which is more than 3+3 = 6), while the singular will produce more when added (e.g. 1x1 = 1 but 1+1 = 2 is the greater); but the duad is a medium between one and true multiple numbers which start at three because neither addition or multiplication results in a greater sum (2x2 and 2+2 both equalling 4).

premise and its conclusion: for example, all humans use reason; I am a human; therefore I use reason.

But we can also see this in the most profound myths of antiquity: for example the myth of Kronos, Rhea and Zeus. Kronos (the name comes from "pure mind") stands for the major premise, the abiding aspect of truth, who swallows his offspring since the abiding does not itself proceed; Rhea ("flowing") stands for the minor premise, the proceeding aspect of truth, which on its own is detached from the major premise and introduces the "other" – the Goddess desires that her offspring live, and so hides Zeus immediately after his birth and gives Kronos a stone in his place. Zeus ("through which") stands for the conclusion, the new manifestation of truth which only arises when the major and minor premises have generated it by their mixing. These three intellectual divinities play out the pattern of bound-infinite-mixed within the intellectual sphere. The conclusion of the pattern is the creation of the manifested universe, for Zeus is the Demiurge.

Finally, the lowest line of four, represents the manifested cosmos: this cosmos has four constituents: the three orders (soul, nature, and the mundane) and the pure passive potential of matter. Ancient physiologists have always associated actual manifestation with the number four, using the four elements – earth, air, fire and water – as their symbolic names. Modern science, too, finds that the basic forces and building blocks of the universe come in fours (for example the four atomic forces known as strong, weak, gravity and electromagnetic; and the four DNA bases - A, T, C, and G). In geometry, too, the simplest solid figure has four sides (this being the three-faced pyramid with its base.

Thus the Pythagorean hymn says, "Divine number proceeds from the retreats of the undecaying monad, till it arrives at the divine tetrad which produced the mother of all things, the universal recipient, venerable, circularly investing all things with bound, immovable and unwearied and which is denominated the sacred decad, both by the immortal gods and earthborn men."

Chapter Five

The True Earth

Originally a paper presented to the Millennium Trust Conference - In Praise of the Earth - in September 2002. I include it here because it centres on an exploration of Proclus' refinement of Aristotle's theory of causes: the student who has begun to think in terms of the six orders will see that the six causes given here have clear correspondences to the characteristics of the orders. A postscript is added to the original paper which looks at this.

O Mother Earth, of Gods and men the source,
Endu'd with fertile, all-destroying force;
All-parent, bounding, whose prolific pow'rs
Produce a store of beauteous fruits and flow'rs.
All-various maid, th'immortal world's strong base,
Eternal, blessed, crown'd with every grace.
(Orphic Hymn, XXVI, To Earth)

As Socrates points out in the *Symposium*, when called upon to praise something it is always best to speak the truth, rather than flatter. For an enlightened man this is easy; for the rest of us the attempt must be to draw as close to the truth of the subject as possible. It is in this spirit that I offer these few words.

Why do we need a conference entitled *In Praise of Earth*? Is it because we take joy from the diverse praises that each participant brings to the common feast? Or is it because we think that the Earth is not sufficiently praised in our present culture, and that our conference will address this lack? Perhaps both. The second possibility is strange: if praise accompanies knowledge, how is it that the praise of earth is so muted in our culture which so prides itself on the rapid advance of its sciences?

That praise and knowledge are intertwined is clear: when a musician comes across the work of a new composer which resonates with him, he will investigate the works of the composer and, eventually, he will praise the composer through a loving rendition of his music. Likewise, when we come across a person who awakens love within our heart we want to know everything about that person – who can forget the first evening with a lover, and the intensity of exploration? Eventually the life we live with our beloved becomes – or should become – a praise of the beloved in deed.

Has this happened with our culture which has devoted so much of its time and energy in the exploration of the natural sciences? I think not. Generally speaking our world society's relationship with the earth is characterised by exploitation rather than by love – and while love praises and enlarges, exploitation denigrates and belittles. This can only mean one thing: we do not know the earth, and that our so-called science is in some fundamental way flawed. For all the effort man has put towards exploring the earth since the dawning of the so-called scientific age, it seems that in important ways our understanding of our world has regressed rather than progressed. Let me outline why this is the case. All science is concerned with knowing things through their causes; according to Aristotle (Metaphysics I, 2) everything has four broad causes: a *final cause*, which is the purpose of the thing; an *essential or formal cause*, which is the pre-existing idea of the thing; the *efficient*, which is the maker of the thing; and the *material*, which is the materials from which a thing is made.

To give a brief example of this, we may look at a simple loaf of bread: the final cause, or purpose, of the loaf is to assuage the hunger of its consumers; its essential or formal cause is the idea of the loaf, which may be passed on to its would-be baker encoded as a recipe; its material cause is the flour, yeast, salt, and the other ingredients which go to make up the loaf, together with the heat of the oven. Proclus, many centuries after Aristotle, refined this pattern in order to distinguish between the universal idea and the particular form of any thing as well as to insert an *instrumental cause* between the efficient and the material: to add these to our example, the universal idea of a loaf held in the mind of the baker would be accompanied by a particular form to which any particular loaf would be moulded - to give it a particular size, particular shape, and particular decoration, amongst other things; the sixth cause, the instrumental, would cover all the particular instruments used by the baker - utensils, tins, ovens, and so on. Proclus called the cause which gave particular forms to particular things the *formal cause*, but the cause which is from universal ideas he called *paradigmatic*. If, then, these different causes are truly what makes things to be what they are, the scientist must investigate them, to enable him to know the things as effects of definite causes.

Before we ask whether today's scientists know things in all their causes, we ought to consider briefly the relationship between these various causes. We should be able to discern a hierarchy of causes which, for very obvious reasons, is based on the power of each class of cause. Traditionally this hierarchy was headed by the final cause;

second to the final came the formal; then followed the efficient cause; lastly came the material cause.

Each cause in the hierarchy has the power to bring about causes lower than itself. Let us return to our caused loaf: if no one was ever hungry - in other words, if there was no causal reason for bread - we would not have ideas concerning food, nor would we have recipes (formal causes), nor would we have bakers (efficient causes), nor would we grow grains and yeasts, and gather salt or build ovens (the material causes). Thus we can see that the final cause is the crucial initiating cause of the other classes of cause. It may be a little less obvious why the idea is above the efficient cause in this hierarchy: does not the cook produce the recipe, and is, therefore, to be considered as primary to the formal cause? This is, perhaps, where Proclus' distinction between universal idea and particular form is most useful. It is true that the inventor conceives a particular form from which things can be made: but we do not invent universal ideas. Universals ideas are eternal realities which the mind discovers. Indeed, it is one of the wonders of the human experience that no matter how a powerful political or social system tries to suppress a real idea, it cannot: the idea calls to the thinker, and once discovered the idea possesses the thinker. The weakest cause is the material: no matter how much flour and other ingredients we possess we would never bake a loaf if hunger, recipes or bakers did not exist. The material can never bring into being the final, formal or efficient causes.

Now, what causes does modern science investigate most systematically and assiduously? When today's scientist is asked why something exists, he will normally reply in terms of material and efficient causes. The idea that something exists primarily because of a purpose is alien to his way of thinking; it is equally alien to suggest that universal ideas not only exist but that they are actually the active causes of all manifested things. The orthodox thinker today will explain things in terms of mechanisms, in which the efficient cause and the material cause are the only real elements.[42] Worse than this, most will doubt the reality of

---

[42] This perhaps follows a change in thinking during the time when the old philosophical order was giving way to the new religious order in the second and third centuries C.E. It is noticeable that while the Platonic tradition places the *final cause* first and sees the others emerging from it, the thinkers of the Christian era saw the primary cause as the *efficient* – in other words God was first and foremost a creator, and the ideas and purposes which are the formal and final causes arise out of the "person" of God the father. It is perhaps no surprise that an era which starts with a loss of The One and the promotion of the Demiurge to its place abandons the study of final and formal causes and descends into mere mechanics.

purposes and ideas as independent things - considering them as merely ephemeral constructs of the mind. The entire true nature of reality is thus inverted and the ancient system of philosophy and science, which affirmed purpose and idea as the highest causes, becomes as a foreign language. Once this inversion has occurred, everything moves out of alignment; to give one small example, ancient science tells us that the abstract mind brings into being the brain, while modern science assumes that the physical brain somehow causes the abstract mind.

This is, of course, absurd. When I ask for an explanation of a Beethoven piano sonata, I do not want someone to tell me that everything is explicable in terms of the hammers hitting the strings, or fingers striking the keys: although it would be quite true to say that every sound I hear of the sonata is indeed a result of these things and I could not identify a single note which arises externally to this mechanism.

The great problem with the West's dialogue between its so-called religion and science divide is that proof of a spiritual reality is so often postulated (by the religionist) on the grounds of the known mechanical paradigm being unable to explain certain aspects of manifestation. When the scientist eventually discovers the missing bit of the mechanism, the man of religion retreats further back and casts around for another gap in the mechanism. This process is to misunderstand the nature of causality. From one point of view we can say *that for everything that exists there is a completely mechanical explanation*, in just the same way that for every note I hear of the sonata there is a completely mechanical explanation.

Having said this, however, we can equally well claim that for everything that exists a mechanical explanation is inadequate, since all mechanisms are brought into existence only because of an abstract purpose and a dynamic universal idea. It is the knowledge of these causes which transforms the mechanic into a sage: and this everyone acknowledges in their heart, if not in their conscious philosophy. The great composer and his inspired interpreter are revered; the great piano maker and the piano tuner are, at best, admired. *A science which does not know purposes and universal ideas is, in reality, no science at all*, any more than the human being is a human being without the mind and affectional nature.

Having made our analysis of causes into a four- or six-fold pattern we can, perhaps, reduce it to a simple two-fold one: ideas and purposes can be seen as *divine causes*, because they directly participate in divine nature which is eternal and unmoving; while efficient and material are *necessary causes* because they are determined by the higher ones and are conjoined with the cycles of time. The former causes answer the question *why*, while the latter answer the question *how*. As Plato says (in the *Timaeus*) "It is requisite to distinguish two species of causes; the one necessary, but the other divine. And we should inquire after the divine cause in all things, for the sake of obtaining a blessed life in as great a degree as our nature is capable of receiving it; but we should investigate the necessary cause for the sake of that which is divine. For we should consider, that without these two species of causes, the objects of our pursuit can neither be understood nor apprehended, nor in any other way become participated." In other words the knowledge of final and formal causes bestow on rational beings a happy life, while a knowledge of the efficient and material causes should serve to draw the reasoning being on towards the contemplation of the higher types of cause.

It is not surprising, therefore, that our culture's relationship to the earth is so flawed and that our understanding of Mother Earth is so limited. I believe that much work is required in the proper investigation of earth, and that without this effort we will suffer much from what will seem to be both natural and human disasters.

It is, therefore, necessary to return to the ancient sages in order to re-establish the proper order of causes, and in so doing enable us to speak the truth concerning Earth which will then constitute its true praise.

"There are indeed many and admirable places belonging to the earth," says Socrates (in the *Phaedo*, 108c), "and the earth itself is neither of such a kind, nor of such a magnitude, as those who are accustomed to speak about it imagine." We should note that this is the beginning of one of the last speeches of Socrates who was soon to be obliged to drink the jailor's hemlock. Since a wise man who knows he is about to die does not spend the last moments of his life talking about unworthy things, nor exploring falsity, we may especially trust this exposition of the nature of the earth as being both essential to our own wisdom and true. He continues: "I am persuaded, therefore, in the first place, that if the earth is in the middle of the heavens, and is of a spherical figure, it has no occasion of air, nor of any other such-like necessity, to prevent it from falling: but that the perfect similitude of the heavens to themselves, and the equilibrity of the earth, are sufficient causes of its support. For that which is equally inclined, when placed in the middle of a similar nature, cannot tend more or less to one part than another; but, subsisting on all sides similarly affected, it will remain free from all inclination . . .

but that the earth itself, which is of a pure nature, is situated in the pure heavens, in which the stars are contained, and which most of those who are accustomed to speak about such particulars denominate æther."

We can see from this description, that the earth is a part of the divinely-ordered heavens, each body of which is an image of a god. Indeed, in the *Timaeus* (at 49b) Plato calls the earth the "nurse of all" and (40c) "the first and most ancient of Gods generated within the heavens." If we want to be more specific regarding the divine name of this stable and nourishing goddess we might look at Plato's description in the Phaedrus (246a ff) of the procession of the Gods who follow Zeus – "The army of Gods and dæmons, distributed into eleven parts, follows his course; but Hestia alone remains in the habitation of the Gods." This Goddess, unmoving and yet set in the heavens is referred to by Aristotle, the pupil of Plato, in his treatise *On the World* (ch. 2), even more clearly as being identified with the earth: "But of this order, the life-supporting earth is allotted the middle, which is immovable and stable, she being the Hestia and mother of all-various animals." Now the name Hestia is related to the root "est" which in so many languages in Europe means *is*. In other words the earth is the Goddess which sustains all things in their is-ness - not only those things which are mortal and changeable but also those things which are immortal and unchanging, as Orpheus had sung in his hymn to the Earth (xxvi) "*O Mother Earth, of Gods and men the source . .*"

If this is so we should not imagine the earth to be the merely material things before our senses, for that which is material cannot sustain that which is immaterial. We will see that Socrates' view of the earth is much more than this, for later in the *Phaedo* he says:

> "It is reported then in the first place, that this earth, if any one surveys it from on high, appears like globes covered with twelve skins, various, and distinguished with colours; a pattern of which are the colours found among us, and which our painters use. But there the whole earth is composed from materials of this kind, and such as are much more splendid and pure than our region contains: for they are partly indeed purple, and endued with a wonderful beauty; partly of a golden colour; and partly more white than plaster or snow; and are composed from other colours in a similar manner, and those more in number and more beautiful than any we have ever beheld.

For the hollow parts of this pure earth, being filled with water and air, exhibit a certain species of colour, shining among the variety of other colours in such a manner, that one particular various form of the earth continually presents itself to the view. Hence, whatever grows in this earth grows analogous to its nature, such as trees, and flowers, and fruits: and again, its mountains and stones possess a similar perfection and transparency, and are rendered beautiful through various colours; of which the stones so much honoured by us in this place of our abode are but small parts, such as sardin-stones, jaspers, and emeralds, and all of this kind. But there nothing subsists which is not of such a nature as I have described; and there are other things far more beautiful than even these. But the reason of this is because the stones there are pure, and not consumed and corrupted, like ours, through rottenness and salt, from a conflux of various particulars, which in our places of abode cause filthiness and disease to the stones and earth, animals and plants, which are found among us.

But this pure earth is adorned with all these, and with gold and silver, and other things of a similar nature: for all these are naturally apparent, since they are both numerous and large, and are diffused every where throughout the earth; so that to behold it is the spectacle of blessed spectators. This earth too contains many other animals and men, some of whom inhabit its middle parts; others dwell about the air, as we do about the sea; and others reside in islands which the air flows round, and which are situated not far from the continent. And in one word, what water and the sea are to us, with respect to utility, that air is to them: but what air is to us, that æther is to the inhabitants of this pure earth. But the seasons there are endued with such an excellent temperament, that the inhabitants are never molested with disease, and live for a much longer time than those who dwell in our regions; and they surpass us in sight, hearing, and prudence, and every thing of this kind, as much as air excels water in purity - and æther, air.

And besides this, they have groves and temples of the Gods, in which the Gods dwell in reality; and likewise oracles and divinations, and sensible perceptions of the Gods, and such-like associations with them. The sun too, and moon, and stars, are seen by them such as they really are; and in every other respect their felicity is of a correspondent nature."

Now this is a description of the earth as seen from its eternal standpoint: what stands out – apart from its beauty and majesty – is its divine nature: the twelve skins are indicative of the twelve mundane Gods, through whose powers and involvement the world is made and continues as it is. The earth described here, too, is inhabited by intelligent beings who know things as they are – in other words in the final and essential causes – and who are in true communication with Divinity.

When human scientists change their perspective and pursue the divine and intelligent reasons of the earth they will be able to say with Synesius, "that incorruptible intellect which is wholly an emanation of divinity, is totally diffused through the whole world, convolves the heavens, and preserves the universe with which it is present distributed in various forms. That one part of this intellect is distributed among the stars, and becomes, as it were, their charioteer; but another part among the angelic choirs; and another part is bound in a terrestrial form."

The mechanisms of this world, when viewed as the means whereby divine causes are brought into material manifestation will not lose their miraculous beauty, nor will we lose our technological wizardry: in fact quite the opposite. The beauties of the world will deepen, the power we have to draw out of the natural realm new expressions of its potential will double and redouble. And all of this, because we will be able to place our mechanical knowledge and application within a greater context, will be placed in the service of the perfection of the universe as a whole, rather than the selfish interests of intemperate desires.

In brief what I am suggesting is that our science, both formal and our own everyday thinking must re-establish purposes and ideas as things-in-themselves, and not regard them as products of the thinker. If this is done our religious life will begin to pay due reverence to all things as being full of living divinity. For how could we consider anything as purely passive and exploitable material when it is seen as the outworking of eternal purposes and ideas: for these things do not produce externally but in some mysterious manner enter into their own creations; thus does Proclus say that "all things are full of the Gods."

Once our thinking has returned to the true order of causes as understood by all sages in all times and lands, we may with the most truthful Orpheus sing of the Earth –

"Eternal, blessed, crown'd with every grace."

Postscript: It is worth looking again at the six causes outlined above. Proclus (in his *Commentary on the Timaeus*, I, 263) names the causes as final, paradigmatic, efficient, instrumental (or organic), the formal and the material. In effect he divides the efficient into the efficient and instrumental, and the ideal into the paradigmatic and the formal. He says that the (manifested) universe, not being real being, but that which is generated has the instrumental, formal and material as its immediate causes, and that these three arise from the higher three of final, paradigmatic and efficient.

The *final cause* of any thing can be traced back to a general purpose – to manifest some aspect of the goodness which is inherent in being; as such we can say that the *Intelligible order* provides the final cause of all things.

The *paradigmatic* or *ideal cause* is the universal pattern of the effect: it is clearly a result of the *Intelligible-Intellectual order* from which all the dynamic ideas of the universe spring.

The *efficient cause* is the maker of the thing: it is the idealising and creative power which looks to the final and ideal cause, is inspired by them, and puts them into objective manifestation. We can see that Zeus, as creator of the manifested universe is the great efficient cause of all. Thus we can correlate the efficient cause with the *Intellectual order.*

The *instrumental cause* is that which the efficient cause uses as its intermediary between itself and the lower orders of natural types (or individuated forms) and matter: the soul acts as the instrument to the intellect, and as the intermediary between the stable Intellectual order and the moving order of nature. The soul is called self-motive, and therefore it clearly moves, but its motion starts from its own essence, and for this reason this essence must have something of the unmoving characteristic of the order of the efficient cause. For this reason we can see the instrumental causes correspond to the *order of soul.*

The *formal cause* (and here we have to be careful not to mix the name up with the original Aristotelian formal cause, which can be seen as more paradigmatic than this lower formal cause) is the actual type which stands immediately above the actualised material thing – it is the universal form carried down to the point at which it will make a particular thing manifest: not *that* cup but *this* cup. We can correlate this formal cause with the *order of nature* which provides the mundane realm with a series of appropriate types which interact with matter.

Lastly the *material cause* clearly correlates with the *mundane order* which provides the matter from which the never-ending series of the particular things arises. As each thing decays, having lost its previous form, so its constituent parts are taken over by a newly emerging material thing.

Appendix 1

Proclus on Procession and Reversion

Throughout this book we have affirmed a basic metaphysical law – that causes and effects are related. L J Rosan in his exceptional work on Proclus introduces his chapter on Ontology with the following summary of what the metaphysician must discover:[43]

> The major ontological problem that is raised by Cosmology is: "What does it mean for something *to be something else?*" But since the answer to this question involves a series of relationships, it gives rise to an even more abstract problem: "What does it mean for something *to be related* to something else?" This requires us to answer the most abstract problem of all: "What does it mean for something *to be?*"

We have looked briefly at the question of being – that every being depends upon some underlying *unity*; that it must have a stable *boundary* to make it exactly what it is; and that it must have a *power* to maintain its characteristic identity for an appropriate measure – whether that measure is eternal, or temporal. We have also explored the concept of participation as a procession together with its accompanying concept, conversion. But it may be useful to consider Rosan's first two questions a little more deeply – what does it mean for something to be something else? And what does it mean for something to be related to something else?

These are, of course, concepts we use all the time in our thinking, but we rarely give such basic questions our conscious attention. So, for example, when we say that Socrates is a man, what do we mean? We really mean that there is an idea of man in which Socrates in some manner participates. The relationship between man and Socrates is a stable one, but also asymmetrical – that is to say, the idea of man does not participate in Socrates, only that Socrates participates in the idea of man. The idea of man, therefore, has become Socrates, but at the same time remains in itself, and not Socrates.

In truth, we must go beyond Rosan's fundamental questions and ask how does something as simple and transcendent as The One give rise to the complex universe around us, with its innumerable things both

---

[43] *The Philosophy of Proclus*, The Prometheus Trust, Westbury, 2010, p. 58

material and immaterial and their extraordinary variety of characteristics?

The Platonic answers to these questions are succinctly presented in Proclus' *Elements of Theology*, and some important metaphysical axioms are laid down in a small section of six propositions which (with their accompanying rational proofs) outline the way procession takes place. He then follows this group with eight further propositions which deal with reversion (or conversion). Let us take these fourteen propositions one at a time:

25 "Every thing perfect proceeds to the generation of those things which it is able to produce, imitating the One Principle of all."

Proclus' proof of this assertion rests on the nature of the "One Principle of all" – which is The Good. One of the primary characteristics of the Good is that of perfection (of course – we are intuitively aware that anything which is not perfect cannot be described as absolutely good). And, says, Proclus, the more perfect anything is, the more it is productive – even in animal life, we can see that as a living thing reaches its maturity (its completeness, or perfection) so it become generative of further lives. It is this principle of generation through perfection to which Diotima refers in the *Symposium* at the end of her reported speech to Socrates.[44] It is the nature of the good, therefore, to be unenvyingly giving: Plato, writing in the *Timaeus* (29e) notes of the Demiurgus, or creator of the manifested universe, that "the creator was good; but in that which is good envy never subsists about anything which has being. Hence, as he was entirely void of envy, he was willing to produce all things as much as possible similar to himself. . . he fabricated the universe; that thus it might be a work naturally the most beautiful and the best."

Since every effect retains something of its cause,[45] it follows that the series of entities which arise from this initial "One Principle of all" carry with them to a greater or lesser extent the impulse to generate and produce. Procession is the movement from cause to effect, and from these primary effects onwards to subsequent effects – and thus we see that the power of procession is inherent in all beings.

---

[44] 212a

[45] Or, looking at this from the cause downwards, as Proclus does in proposition 18 – "Every thing which imparts existence to others, is itself that primarily which it communicates to the natures that are supplied by it with existence."

26 "Every cause which is productive of other things, itself abiding in itself, produces the natures posterior to itself, and such as are successive."

Two important points of this proposition should be noted here: firstly, that a true cause *abides in itself*: as I have emphasized throughout my section of this book, real ideas are not affected by the adventures of their effects – the destruction, for example, of some or even all material instances of beauty makes no impression on the idea of beauty. This is because, as Proclus says, a cause abides in itself – it is not distributed and broken up into its effects. We should be aware, therefore, that what we are considering in our exploration of procession and reversion is metaphysical causes; and we can see the material cause is often regarded as less than a true cause: in our example on page 144, if the material cause of a loaf of bread is collectively the flour, yeast and water from which it is made, it can hardly be said to abide in itself and is, of course, distributed into its effect, so that what happens to the loaf happens also to its ingredients.

The second point is that an original cause is productive firstly of its immediate effects and then subsequently of further effects *through the medium* of those primary effects. It is worth reading Plato's description of the Demiurgus' creation in the *Timaeus* (from 27c to 42c) where we can see this intellectual creator God first bringing into activity the powers of the junior gods, and then using these powers as intermediaries to bring into being such natures as populate the manifest worlds bounded by time. We will see deeper implications of this when we consider proposition 38.

27 "Every producing cause, on account of its perfection, and abundance of power, is productive of secondary natures."

This is Proclus' summary of the basic law of procession – and in his supporting proof he asserts that it is *because* this causal power arises from perfection that it itself remains unaffected and unmoved by its effects: the obverse of this is, of course, that things that act as causes because of their own imperfections are necessarily moved – for to produce something to address a lack is (if successful) to change oneself into a better condition.

28 "Every producing cause gives subsistence to things similar to itself, prior to such as are dissimilar."

Here is the great key to the unfolding of the universe from the First Principle of all – similarity.

We have already seen how important it is to understand the procession from The One to the last of things as stemming from an overflowing perfection of Good. Everything which arises after The One is, therefore, an effect of goodness – a particular instance of goodness which can be traced back to the absolutely transcendent Good. But if this is the case, then if there were a vacuum at any point between the First Principle and the ultimate expression of that Principle in the final receptivity of matter, then such a vacuum would have to be, by definition, a complete lack of goodness – and we would have to see such a vacuum as somehow more powerful than the super-abundant Good. The "hole" in the universe of goodness would, in effect, be a boundary to the Good, resistant to its power. But this is impossible, because the vacuum to resist the Good, it, too, would have to have a power, and this would have to be derived from some principle: we would then have to look for a higher principle which supplied both the Good and the Vacuum with their respective powers. But this more powerful principle itself would have to be perfect (in order to generate both the Good and the Vacuum) and so all we have done is find something which we must now call The Good and absolutely transcendent, and mark our original "Good" down as an effect of *this* transcendent.

The universe is then a fullness of Good, without a vacuum: but what does this mean metaphysically? Clearly, we are not concerned with spatial gaps, but as Proclus says in his treatise on *Fate, Providence and That which is Within our Power*,[46] "the progression of beings much more than the situation of bodies, leaves no vacuum." The gradual unfolding of being is through *qualitative separation* – as each effect emerges from a cause, and as that effect becomes a causal agent for further effects, so there must be no great jumps in gradation of goodness; for such jumps would be metaphysical vacuums.

So the first effect to emerge from any cause is almost the same as its cause – almost but not quite the same, since there would be no purpose in producing a repetition of goodness. So just as that which is closest to a fire is almost as hot as the fire itself, so that which is closest metaphysically to a causal agent is most similar to it. And, as we have seen in proposition 26, the same agent acts as a cause to subsequent effects through the medium of its first effects: but these secondary effects are less like the cause than its primary effects because of the

---

[46] This treatise is included in *Essays and Fragments of Proclus*, TTS vol. XVIII, p.18.

intervention of the intermediary causes. Again, we can see a similar process in mundane life as the children of a mother and father are most similar to them, but subsequent generations become less and less like those original ancestors, as more and more generations of parents intervene as generative causes.

In this way the universe is extended from the One Principle of all, each step outwards and downwards being the minimum required to give distinctness to the newly emerged effect. And just as when we design an electrical installation we must provide a means whereby power can be continuously conducted, so it is with the universe, which can be seen as a system which allows goodness to be conducted from its originating source to its ultimate manifestation in matter.

29 "Every progression is effected through a similitude of secondary to first natures."

If *perfection* is the characteristic which marks the cause, *similarity* is the characteristic which marks the effect. Without this principle, the correspondence between cause and effect would become unreliable and disordered. Similarity is what allows the idea to reside in its effect (while, of course, still abiding in its transcendent purity). An interesting application of this concept is used by Socrates in the final proof of the immortality of the soul in the *Phaedo* – the so-called argument from essence. Briefly, Socrates suggests that the soul has an essential quality of life (it gives life to otherwise inanimate matter when present to body, and when it withdraws from the body, the matter is returned to its inanimate state); but, he says, when death approaches the body, the soul must retreat and go elsewhere. For death is unlike the soul, and psyche could not abide in a dead body – it then departs to Hades to continue living, but no longer in a terrestrial state.

30 "Every thing which is produced from a certain thing without a medium, abides in its producing cause, and proceeds from it."

The power of similarity now begins to show its extraordinary worth: we have seen that similarity allows the cause to reside in its effect through procession; but with this proposition, we can see that, equally, the effect also abides in the cause, through the same power of similarity; for underlying the whole metaphysical scheme of the universe is the truth that every effect is held in its producer causally. As stated in the discussion on proposition 28, an single step from cause to effect implies two things – sameness and distinction. The distinction, being mixed with the same, produces similarity: distinction forces procession away from the cause, but sameness allows the effect to abide in the cause. We can look at it through the negative argument: if an effect had no distinction it would be entirely the same as its cause, and would not proceed, but only abide in it; and if an effect had no sameness but only consisted of its distinction, there would be no relationship between cause and effect, and all order would be destroyed – indeed, it would mean that the procession which took place between any cause and its effect would create a vacuum.

31 "Every thing which proceeds from a certain thing essentially, is converted to that from which it proceeds."

Let us reaffirm the original cause of procession: *an unenvying overflowing of good.* When, therefore, something is brought into being by a cause, we can say that the effect is given its good through the activity of that cause – for the whole purpose of the causal action is to pass on that goodness which the cause is capable of communicating to its effect. Now all things desire good, and since the cause has delivered to the effect goodness adapted to that particular effect, the effect must find its goodness in its own cause. The desire for good, then, leads the effect which has proceeded from the cause to *revert to that cause.*

32 "All conversion is effected through the similitude of the things converted to that to which they are converted."

The reversion (or conversion) of the proceeded effect back to its abiding cause can only be brought about through the commonality which the cause and effect share – remembering that it was the difference (or distinction) which forced the procession out from the cause. So not only can we see that the procession of the good outwards into wider and wider manifestation is ordered through similarity, but also that reversion is governed by the same law of similarity. Indeed, we might say that *the whole metaphysical universe is articulated through similarity.*

33 "Every thing which proceeds from a certain thing and is converted to it, has a circular energy."

This circular energy conjoins causes and effects, and those who see the universe and all its parts in the light of this energy, are freed from the illusion of separation in which reality is reduced to a powder of discrete particles. Proclus in his supporting proof indicates that the circular energy is from the One Principle of all and back to it, but that it is continually imitated at every metaphysical level.

34 'Every thing which is converted according to nature, makes its conversion to that from which also it had the progression of its proper hypostasis."

The hypostasis (lit. "that which stands under") is the very substance of the effect. This proposition may appear to be a repetition of the thirty-first, but the emphasis here is upon the nature ("phusis") of the thing which is reverting – it therefore rests on the inherent impulse of the effect to return to its cause because of its own appetite for its own good.

35 "Every thing caused, abides in, proceeds from, and returns, or is converted to, its cause."

Drawing the various preceding propositions together, Proclus shows in his supporting proofs that the triad of abiding-proceeding-converting is a complete and unified action, no aspect of which can be missing if the metaphysics of reality is to be perfect. While it is tempting to see the threefold principle as a process of three steps, we must remember that all three are simultaneously present within every metaphysical cause and effect relationship.

36 "Of all things which are multiplied according to progression, the first are more perfect than the second, the second than those posterior to them, and after the same manner successively."

Of course, this is because the cause of an effect is always closer to the good, and therefore great in perfection and power. When a series of causes and effects are unfolded, the further "down" any particular term lies in the series, the further away it is from the originating good.

37 "Of all things which subsist according to conversion, the first are more imperfect than the second, and the second than those that follow; but the last are the most perfect."

The converse, however, is also true – in the series of causes and effects, the more something reverts towards the originating principle, the more it is filled with perfection and power. So that in the last phase of conversion, the returning effect is most similar to the goodness and power of its causes.

38   "Every thing which proceeds from certain numerous causes, is converted through as many causes as those are through which it proceeds, and all conversion is through the same things as those through which progression is effected."

The whole metaphysical universe can be seen as a series of radiating moves out from the mysterious and all-powerful centre, which is The One or The Good.   Each move takes the good through orderly transformations in a chain of causes and effects, so that eventually what started out as a single, simple, and transcendent good (or a single, simple and transcendent unity) is expressed as a multiplex and complex manifestation, which is always moving back towards its source.

As we have seen, any particular thing along this chain reverts to its immediate cause, because it is this cause which gave it its particular good.   But the cause of that effect is also seeking to revert to its cause, which in turn is seeking to return to its own cause – and so on, until the One Principle of all is reached.   For any thing, therefore to return to The Good, it must follow the causal chain, with, as Proclus says, as many conversions as there are processions between it and its ultimate source.

Some commentators have suggested that in these conversions the returning entity regains what has been lost in its procession out from the source.   This is true, although we should be aware that we can equally well see the conversion as losing what has been added in that procession – that the conversion is always to simplicity.   Thus Proclus in his *Commentary on the Timaeus*, when discussing the return of the human soul, says,[47]

> "For it is necessary that the soul which is hurled like seed into the realms of generation, should lay aside the stubble and bark, as it were, which she obtained from being disseminated into these fluctuating realms; and that purifying herself from every thing circumjacent, she should become an intellectual flower and fruit, delighting in an intellectual life, instead of doxastic nutriment, and pursuing the uniform and simple energy of the period of sameness, instead of the abundantly wandering motion of the period which is characterized by difference."

The reader will, I hope, see how important it is to get our metaphysics clear and properly ordered – because our ethics and re-ascent to our source are intimately bound up with our understanding of them.

---

[47] *Commentary on the Timaeus*, 330A, TTS vol. XVI, p. 992.

Appendix 2

Proclus' Elements of Theology

Propositions 1 – 6

The following translation of the first six propositions of Proclus' *Elements of Theology* is that of Thomas M Johnson, the editor of *The Platonist*, and a leading light in the small but significant band of Platonists who lived and worked at the end of the nineteenth and beginning of the twentieth centuries in the United States. Johnson's publication of *The Elements of Theology* was soundly based on that of Thomas Taylor, whose memory Johnson revered; he wrote in the introduction "In translating the Metaphysical Elements I have spent many intensely laborious but very pleasant and extremely profitable hours. The translation is based on Taylor's, but it would be an act of injustice to him to call my version a revision of his, though my indebtedness to him is large, and cheerfully acknowledged."

Propositions 1 to 5 – On The One

Proposition 1: *Every multitude partakes in some respect of The One*

For if it in no way or degree participates of The One, neither will the whole be one, nor each of the many things from which multitude arises, but each multitude will originate from certain or particular things, and this will continue *ad infinitum*. And of these infinites each will be again infinite multitude. For, if multitude partakes in no respect of any one, neither as a whole nor through any of its parts, it will be in every respect indeterminate. Each of the many, whichever you may assume, will be one or not one; and if not one will be either many or nothing. But if each of the many is nothing, that likewise which arises from these will be nothing. If each is many, each will consist of infinites without limit. But this is impossible. For there is no being constituted of infinites without limit, since there is nothing greater than the infinite itself; and that which consists of all is greater than each particular thing. Neither is any thing composed of nothing. Every multitude therefore partakes in some respect of The One.

Proposition 2: *Every thing which partakes of The One is alike one and not one.*

For though it is not The One itself - since it participates of The One and is therefore other than it is - it experiences The One through participation, and is thus able to become one. If therefore it is nothing besides The One, it is one alone, and will not participate of The One but will be The One itself. But if it is something other than The One, which is not The One but a participant of it, it is alike one and non-one, - one being, indeed, since it partakes of oneness, but not oneness itself. This therefore is neither The One itself, nor that which The One is. But, since it is one and at the same time a participant of The One, and on this account not one *per se*, it is alike one and not one, because it is something other than The One. And so far as it is multiplied it is not one; and so far as it experiences a privation of number or multitude it is one. Every thing, therefore, which participates of The One is alike one and not one.

Proposition 3: *Every thing which becomes one, becomes so by the participation of The One, and is one so far as it experiences the participation of The One.*

For if the things which are not one become one, they doubtless become so by a harmonious alliance and association with each other, and experience the presence of The One, though they are not that which The One is. Hence they participate of The One, so far as they allow themselves to become one. But if they are already one, they will not become one: for that which is, does not become that which it already is. But if they become one from that which was previously not one, they will possess The One, since a certain one was ingenerated in their nature. And this ingenerated one must be derived from The One itself. Every thing, therefore, which becomes one, becomes so by the participation of The One, *etc.*

Proposition 4: *Every thing which is united is different from The One itself.*

For if it is united it will participate in a certain respect of The One, so far as it is rightly said to be united. That, however, which is a participant of The One is both one and not one. But The One itself is not both one and not one: for if this was so, again the one which is in it would have both of these, and this would take place *ad infinitum*, if there was no One itself at which it is possible to stop; but every thing being one and not one, there will be something united, which is different from The One. For if The One is the same as the united, it will be infinite multitude. And in a similar manner each of the things of which the united consists will be infinite multitude. Every thing, therefore, which is united is different from The One itself.

Proposition 5: *All multitude is posterior to The One.*

For if multitude is prior to The One, The One indeed will participate of multitude, but multitude which is prior will not participate of The One, since prior to the existence of The One that multitude was. For it does not participate of that which is not: because a participant of The One is one and at the same time not one - but, on the hypothesis, The One will not yet subsist, that which is first being multitude. But it is impossible that there should be a certain multitude which in no respect whatever participates of The One. Multitude, therefore, is not prior to The One. But if multitude and The One subsist simultaneously, they will be naturally co-ordinate with each other, and intimately related. Nothing in time prohibits this, since neither is The One essentially many, nor is multitude The One, because they are directly opposite to each other by nature, if neither is prior or posterior to the other. Hence multitude essentially will not be one, and each of the things which are in it will not be one, and this will be the case to infinity, which is impossible. Multitude, therefore, according to its own nature participates of The One, and there is no thing of it which is not one. For if it is not one it will be an infinite, consisting of infinites, as has been demonstrated. Hence it entirely participates of The One. If therefore The One, which is essentially one, in no possible respect participates of multitude, multitude will be wholly posterior to The One - participating indeed of The One, but not being participated of it. But if The One participates of multitude, subsisting indeed as one according to its essence, but as not one according to participation, The One will be multitude, just as multitude is united by reason of The One. The One therefore will communicate with multitude, and multitude with The One. But things which coalesce and communicate with each other in a certain respect, if they are impelled together by another, that is prior to them: but if they themselves harmonize they are not antagonistic to each other. For opposites do not hasten to each other. If therefore The One and multitude are oppositely divided, and multitude so far as it is multitude is not one, and The One so far as it is one is not multitude, neither will one of these subsisting in the other be one and at the same time two. And if there is something prior to them, which impels them to harmonize, this will be either many or nothing. But neither will it be many, lest multitude should be prior to The One, nor will it be nothing. For how could nothing impel together those things which are something or many? It is therefore one alone. For this one is not many, lest there should be a progression to infinity. It is therefore The One itself, and all multitude proceeds from The One itself.

Proposition 6 – On Unity

Proposition 6: *Every multitude consists either of things united, or of unities.*

It is evident that each of things many will not be itself multitude alone, and, again, that each part of this will not be multitude alone. But if it is not multitude alone, it is either united or unities. And if indeed it partakes of The One it is united; but if it consists of things of which that which is primarily united consists, it will be unities. For if The One itself exists, there is also that which primarily participates of it, and which is primarily united. But this consists of unities: for if it consists of things united, again, things united consist of certain things, and this will be the case to infinity. It is necessary, however, that what is primarily united should consist of unities. And thus we have discovered what we proposed at first, *viz.* that every multitude consists either of things united, or of unities.

Notes on Propositions

Pr 1: "If each is many, each will consist of infinites without limit. But this is impossible." It is impossible for each manifold thing to consist of actual infinites, because this would preclude the possibility of thought, since pure infinity cannot be comprehended, and a thing made up of infinites would be incomprehensible for every infinite which it included.

Pr 4: "For if it is united it will participate in a certain respect of The One, so far as it is rightly said to be united. [See pr. 3] That, however, which is a participant of The One is both one and not one. [See pr. 2]"

Pr 5: "For it does not participate of that which is not: because a participant of The One is one and at the same time not one [pr. 2]- but, on the hypothesis, The One will not yet subsist, that which is first being multitude. But it is impossible that there should be a certain multitude which in no respect whatever participates of The One. [pr. 1]"

Pr 6: E R Dodds rightly comments on this proposition: "The argument is simple and seemingly unimportant; but Proclus has tacitly imported into it a metaphysical interpretation which has far reaching consequences for his system." Put as simply as possible, if all things participate in the One, they must either be simple unities which imply plurality, or multiplicities which imply unity and are therefore ultimately analysable into simple unities: just as physical chemicals are either elements (*i.e.* simple unities) or compounds (multiplicities which include simple elements). In this system, the simple unities which imply plurality but are not themselves plurality are the Gods, while the One in which they participate is, of course, God.

Further Reading

The chief writings used as quotes throughout this book are:

Plato
> *The Parmenides*, trans. T Taylor in the Works of Plato III, TTS vol. XI.
> *The Timaeus*, trans. T Taylor in the Works of Plato II, TTS vol. X.
> *The Republic*, trans. T Taylor in the Works of Plato I, TTS vol. IX
> *The Phaedo*, trans. T Taylor in the Works of Plato IV, TTS vol. XII
> For other dialogues and epistles see our catalogue at the end of this book.

Proclus
> *The Theology of Plato*, trans. T Taylor, TTS vol. VIII
> *Commentary on the Parmenides*, trans. T Taylor, parts given in Works of Plato III, TTS vol. XI; full translation Morrow & Dillon, Princeton UP, 1987, Princeton.
> *The Elements of Theology*, trans. T Taylor, TTS vol. I. More modern translations include those of T M Johnson (pub. as *Proclus' Metaphysical Elements*, Osceola, 1909.) Also available is the translation of E R Dodds, Clarendon Press, 1933: a revised version of this is still in print.
> *Commentary on the Timaeus*, trans. T Taylor, TTS vols. XV & XVI.

Plotinus
> *The Enneads*, The most important treatises published in Collected Writings of Plotinus, trans. T Taylor, TTS vol. III.

Modern sources for a view of the last phases of Platonic writings:

R Chlup: *Proclus: An Introduction*, Cambridge UP, 2012.
L J Rosan: *The Philosophy of Proclus*, Cosmos, NY, 1949 but reprinted in 2010 by the Prometheus Trust.
Neoplatonic Philosophy. Introductory Readings. Trans. and ed. by John M. Dillon and Lloyd P. Gerson, Hackett Publishing Co., Indianapolis, 2004
J Gregory: *The Neoplatonists – a Reader* , Routledge (2nd edition 2002)
R T Wallis: *Neoplatonism*, Hackett Pub Co. (2nd edition 1995)

A Philosophic Glossary

Terms used in the translations of Thomas Taylor of the works of Plato, Aristotle, Proclus and others. These explanations are largely drawn from Taylor's own glossaries given in *The Works of Plato* (see TTS IX), *The Theology of Plato* (TTS VIII), and his *Dissertation on the Philosophy of Aristotle* (to be published as TTS XXVIII); in these volumes the Greek usually accompanies the terms. Some amendments and additions are given here in recognition of the changing use of English words since Taylor's time.

ACCIDENT: That which is not of the essential nature of a thing. Thus in a man reason is essential, but to be red-haired is accidental.

ACROAMATIC and SYNTAGMATIC DOCTRINES, are doctrines which require greater study than others, due to their subtle and hidden nature.

ALLIATION. Change in quality.

ANAGOGIC, Leading on high; or that which draws towards divinity.

ANGER. An appetite directed to the avengement of incidental molestations; especially that faculty of the soul which subsists between reason and desire and which seeks to direct the latter in accord with the former – from this point of view a faculty which seeks to ordinate the self, and its environment.

The ATTENTIVE POWER OF THE SOUL. This power investigates and perceives whatever is transacted in man; and says, I understand, I think, I opine, I am angry, I desire. This attentive part of the soul, also, passes through all the rational, irrational, and vegetable or physical powers. In short, this power is *the one* of the soul, which follows all the other powers and energizes together with them. For we should not be able to know all these, and to apprehend in what they differ from each other, unless we contained *a certain indivisible nature*, which has a subsistence above the common sense, and which prior to opinion, desire, and will, knows all that these know and desire, according to an *indivisible* mode of apprehension.

CAPACITY. Is a perfect preparation of essence, and an unimpeded promptitude to energize, prolific of energy. Capacity is that which stands between essence and energy: in eternal things the capacity of an essence is ever-proceeding, while in temporal things a power is said to be *in capacity* in contrast to being *in energy* when it is not yet manifesting. Taylor explains IN ENERGY in these words: "A subsistence in energy is twofold. For it is either as a whole *subsisting* that which it is, as a man or a house; or as that which has its being in *a tendency to existence*, or *in becoming to be*, as a contest and a day; for we say that these are in energy when they are."

CAUSES: There are sixty-four modes of causes according to Aristotle. For every cause is either essential or accidental; and these subsist in a twofold respect. For they subsist either proximately or remotely; and thus produce four modes. All these again have a twofold subsistence; for they are either simple or complex; and thus they produce eight modes. These again, have a twofold subsistence; for they are either in energy, or in capacity; and consequently produce sixteen modes. And because causes are denominated in a fourfold respect; for they are either material, or formal, or efficient, or final; hence there are in all sixty-four modes. Taylor further elucidates causes by carefully translating them in these terms: ON ACCOUNT OF WHICH; WITH REFERENCE TO WHICH; THROUGH WHICH; ACCORDING TO WHICH; FROM WHICH; OR IN WHICH; By the first of these terms, Plato is accustomed to denominate the final cause; by the second the paradigmatic; by the third the demiurgic; by the fourth the instrumental; by the fifth form; and by the sixth matter. This six-fold analysis of cause may be seen as a refinement of Aristotle's fourfold scheme: Aristotle's formal cause is thus divided into universal and particular as the paradigmatic and form; his efficient cause is divided into universal and particular as the demiurgic and instrumental.

COMPOSITE, I have used the word composite instead of *compounded*, because the latter rather denotes the mingling than the contiguous union of one thing with another, which the former, through its derivation from the Latin word *compositus,* solely denotes.

DEMIURGUS, Zeus (Jove or Jupiter) the artificer of the universe. Taylor also gives DEMIURGUS OF WHOLES - the artificer of the universe is thus denominated, because he produces the universe so far as it is a *whole,* and likewise all the wholes it contains, by his own immediate energy; other subordinate powers co-operating with him in the production of parts. Hence he produces the universe *totally* and *at once.*

DESIRE, Is an irrational appetite solely directed to external objects, and to the gratification arising from the possession of them.

DIANOËTIC. This word is derived from διανοια (dianoia), or that power of the soul which reasons scientifically, deriving the principles of its reasoning from intellect. Plato is so uncommonly accurate in his diction, that this word is very seldom used by him in any other than its primary sense. Taylor also gives DIANOIA, (from whence *dianoetic*) as the discursive energy of reason; or according to its most accurate signification, it is that power of the soul which reasons scientifically, deriving the principles of its reasoning from intellect, or the power which sees truth intuitively.

THE DIVINE, το θειον, is *being* subsisting in conjunction with *The One*. For all things except *The One, viz.* essence, life and intellect are considered by Plato as suspended from and secondary to the gods. For the gods do not subsist in, but prior to, these, which they also produce and connect, but are not characterized by these. In many places, however, Plato calls the participants of the gods by the names of the gods. For not only the Athenian guest in the *Laws*, but also Socrates in the *Phædrus*, calls a divine soul a god. "For," says he "all the horses and charioteers of *the gods* are good," *etc.* And afterwards, still more clearly, he adds, "And this is the life of *the gods.*" And not only this, but he also denominates those natures gods, that are always united to the gods, and which, in conjunction with them, give completion to one series. He also frequently calls dæmons gods, though according to essence, they are secondary to, and subsist about, the gods. For in the *Phædrus, Timæus,* and other dialogues, he extends the appellation of the gods as far as to dæmons. And what is still more paradoxical than all this, he does not refuse to call some men gods; as, for instance, the Elean Guest in the *Sophista.* From all this, therefore, we must infer, that with respect to the word god, one thing which is thus denominated is simply deity; another is so according to union; a third, according to participation; a fourth, according to contact; and a fifth, according to similitude. Thus every superessential nature is primarily a god; but every intellectual nature is so according to union. And again, every divine soul is a god according to participation; but divine dæmons are gods, according to contact with the gods; and the souls of men obtain this appellation through similitude. Each of these, however, except the first, is, as we have said, rather divine than a god: for the Athenian Guest, in the *Laws*, calls intellect itself divine. But that which is divine is secondary to the first deity, in the same manner as *the united* is to *The One*; *that which is intellectual,* to *intellect*; and *that which is animated,* to *soul.* Indeed, things more uniform and simple always precede; and the series of beings ends in *The One* itself.

DOXASTIC. This word is derived from δοξα (doxa), *opinion*, and signifies that which is apprehended by opinion, or that power which is the extremity of the rational soul. This power knows the universal in particulars, as that *every* man is a rational animal; but it knows not the διοτι (dioti), or *why* a thing is, but only the οτι (oti), or *that* it is. Also defined as the lowest of the human gnostic powers.

The ETERNAL, that which has a never-ending subsistence, without any connection with time; or, as Plotinus profoundly defines it, infinite life at once total and full.

ENTELECHEIA. Is the possession of perfection; and when it is properly asserted of energy, is not asserted of casual energy, but of that which is perfect, and is established according to a subsistence in energy.

EPHESIS. Is the tendency of inanimate natures to their proper good.

FORM (ειδοσ, eidos) Is the internal characteristic of a thing, and subsists according to λογος (logos), considered as a productive principle, which see.

That which is GENERATED. That which has not the whole of its essence or energy subsisting at once, without temporal dispersion.

GENERATION. An essence composite and multiform, and conjoined with time. This is the proper signification of the word; but it is used symbolically by Plato, and also by theologists more ancient than Plato, for the sake of indication. For as Proclus beautifully observes (in MS. Comment. in Parmenidem.), "Fables call the ineffable unfolding into light through causes, generation." "Hence," he adds, "in the Orphic writings, the first cause is denominated time; for where there is generation, according to its proper signification, there also there is time." In his translations of Aristotle Taylor says that GENERATION "is *universally* the whole of a visible nature, as opposed to an incorporeal and invisible nature. It also *particularly* denotes the sublunary region."

GUEST. The word, in its more ample signification in the Greek, denoted a *stranger*, but properly implies one who receives another, or is himself received at an entertainment. In the following dialogues, therefore, wherever one of the speakers is introduced as a ξενος, I have translated this word *guest*, as being more conformable to the genius of Plato's dialogues, which may be justly called rich mental banquets, and consequently the speakers in them may be considered as so many guests. Hence in the *Timæus*, the persons of that dialogue are expressly spoken of as guests.

HYPARXIS, υπαρξις. The first principle or foundation, as it were, of the essence of a thing. Hence, also, it is the summit of essence. When things are considered as subsisting together in an order, the hyparxis is the leader and unical being of that order. This is in contrast to the *extremity* of the order, which is the lowest level below which only things of a lesser order exist.

HYPOLEPSIS. As dianoia, or the discursive energy of reason, subsists according to terms or boundaries, and is not continued like a physical transition, *the asset and affirmation of the soul according to each boundary, as in one limit, or the assent of the soul to it as true, is hypolepsis.* In other words, hypolepsis is the assent of the soul to each proposition of a syllogism.

IDEA, is an incorporeal cause, exempt from its participants, is an immovable essence, is a paradigm only and truly, and is intelligible to souls from images, but has a causal knowledge of things which subsist according to it. (This distinguishes idea from the universal which is its counterpart within a material object, and also from a human concept formed from the consideration of external objects.)

IDIOM. The characteristic peculiarity of a thing.

The IMMORTAL. According to Plato, there are many orders of immortality, pervading from on high to the last of things; and the ultimate echo, as it were, of immortality, is seen in the perpetuity of the mundane wholes, which according to the doctrine of the Elean Guest in the *Politicus*, they participate from the Father of the universe. For both the being and the life of every body depend on another cause; but since body is not itself naturally adapted to connect, or adorn, or preserve itself. But the immortality of partial souls, such as ours, is more manifest and more perfect than this of the perpetual bodies in the universe; as is evident from the many demonstrations which are given of it in the *Phædo*, and in the 10th book of the *Republic*. For the immortality of partial souls has a more principal subsistence, as possessing in itself the cause of eternal permanency. But prior to both these is the immortality of dæmons; for these neither verge to mortality, nor are filled with the nature of things which are generated and corrupted. More venerable, however, than these, and essentially transcending them, is the immortality of divine souls, which are primarily self-motive, and contain the fountains and principles of the life which is attributed about bodies, and through which bodies participate of renewed immortality. And prior to all these is the immortality of the gods; for Diotima in the *Banquet* does not ascribe an immortality of this kind to dæmons. Hence such an immortality as this is separate and exempt from wholes. For, together with the immortality of the gods, eternity subsists, which is the fountain of all immortality and life, as well as that life which is perpetual, as that which is dissipated into nonentity. In short, therefore, the *divine immortal* is that which is generative and connective of perpetual life. For it is not immortal, as participating of life, but as supplying divine life, and deifying life itself.

IMPARTICIPABLE. That which does not subsist with an inferior nature. Thus imparticipable intellect is an intellect which does not subsist with soul.

INTELLECT. In human beings, is the summit of dianoia, and is that power by the light proceeding from which we perceive the truth of axioms. Of itself considered, it is a being which knows, not by process, but by its very being.

INTELLECTUAL PROJECTION. As the perception of intellect is immediate, being a darting forth, as it were, directly to its proper objects, this direct intuition is expressed by the term *projection*.

The INTELLIGIBLE. This word in Plato and Platonic writers has a various signification: for, in the first place, whatever is exempt from sensibles, and has its essence separate from them, is said to be intelligible, and in this sense soul is intelligible. In the second place, intellect, which is prior to soul, is intelligible. In the third place, that which is more ancient than intellect, which replenishes intelligence, and is essentially perfective of it, is called *intelligible*: and this is the intelligible, which Timæus in Plato places in the order of a paradigm, prior to the demiurgic intellect and intellectual energy. But beyond these is the *divine* intelligible, which is defined according to divine union and hyparxis. For this is intelligible as the object of desire to intellect, as giving perfection to and containing it, and as the completion of being. The highest intelligible, therefore, is that which is the hyparxis of the gods; the second, that which is true being, and the first essence; the third, intellect, and all intellectual life; and the fourth, the order belonging to soul.

LATION is local motion.

LOGISMOS, REASONING. When applied to divinity as by Plato, in the *Timæus*, signifies a distributive cause of things.

LOGOS: see reason.

MONAD, in divine natures is that which contains *distinct*, but at the same time *profoundly-united* multitude, and which produces a multitude exquisitely allied to itself. But in the sensible universe, the first monad is the world itself, which comprehends in itself all the multitude of which it is the cause in conjunction with the cause of all. The second monad is the inerratic sphere. In the third place, the spheres of the planets succeed, each of which is also a monad, comprehending an appropriate multitude. And in the fourth and last place are the spheres of the elements, which are in a similar manner monads. All these monads likewise are denominated ολοτητες, *wholenesses,* and have a perpetual subsistence.

MORPHE. Pertains to the colour, figure, and magnitude of supercifies.

NON-BEING. Is either that which is false, in the same manner as *being* is that which is true; or it is that which in no respect is; or that which in capacity is not.

ORECTIC. The word is derived from *orexis*, appetite. What *orexis* is in animated, that *ephesis* (cf) is in physical inanimate natures.

PARADIGM. A pattern, or that with reference to which a thing is made.

PERMANENCY (στασισ, stasis). The proper word for rest, in Greek, is ηρεμια. And Simplicius justly observes, that not every στασις is ερεμια, but that only which is after motion. This word is employed by Plato in the *Sophista*, to express one of the five genera of being, *viz. essence, permanency*, (στασις), *motion, sameness*, and *difference*; in which place it evidently does not signify rest.

The PERPETUAL. That which subsists forever, but through a connection with time. Also explained by Taylor as "that which subsists always, but is connected with the three parts of time, the past, present, and future. Hence, the fabricator of the world is *eternal*, but the world is *perpetual*."

PHANTASY or *Imagination; a figured intelligence*, because all the perceptions of this power are *inward* and not external, like those of sense, and are accompanied with *figure*. It is the connecting faculty between the purely external senses and the beginnings of reason (*i.e.* opinion) and, as such, it shares some of the characteristics of both, being inward like the rational faculties, but itself irrational like the senses.

A POLITICIAN. This word, as Mr Sydenham justly observes in his notes on the *Rivals*, is of a very large and extensive import, as used by Plato, and the other ancient writers on politics: for it includes all those statesmen or politicians in aristocracies and democracies who were, either for life, or for a certain time, invested with the whole or a part of kingly authority, and the power thereto belonging. See the *Politicus*.

PRE-ELECTION, *i.e.* deliberate choice, is that power which accompanies human reason by which actions can be made to pursue that which is perceived to be good.

PRUDENCE. This word frequently means in Plato and Platonic writers, the habit of discerning what is good in all moral actions, and frequently signifies intelligence, or intellectual perception. The following admirable explanation of this word is given by Iamblichus.

Prudence having a precedaneous subsistence, receives its generation from a pure and perfect intellect. Hence it looks to intellect itself, is perfected by it, and has this as the measure and most beautiful paradigm of all its energies. If also we have any communion with the gods, it is especially effected by this virtue; and through this we are in the highest degree assimilated to them. The knowledge too of such things as are good, profitable, and beautiful, and of the contraries to these, is obtained by this virtue; and the judgment and correction of works proper to be done are by this directed. And in short it is a certain governing leader of men, and of the whole arrangement of their nature; and referring cities and houses, and the particular life of every one, to a divine paradigm, it forms them according to the best similitude; obliterating some things and purifying others. So that prudence renders its possessors similar to divinity. Iamblic. apud. Stob. p. 141.

PSYCHICAL. Pertaining to soul, in the same manner as physical pertains to nature (physis).

QUALITY. Is that which imparts what is apparent in matter, and what is the object of sense.

REASON, λογος (logos). This word in Platonic writers signifies either that inward discursive energy called reasoning; or a certain productive and seminal principle; or that which is indicative and definitive of a thing. Hence λογοι or *reasons* in the soul, are, gnostically producing principles. In more general terms logos also means speech, which is the external expression of reason.

SCIENCE. This word is sometimes defined by Plato to be that which assigns the causes of things; sometimes to be that the subjects of which have a perfectly stable essence; and together with this, he conjoins the assignation of cause from reasoning. Sometimes again he defines it to be that the principles of which are not hypotheses; and, according to this definition, he asserts that there is one science which ascends as far as to the principle of things. For this science considers that which is truly the principle as unhypothetic, has for its subject true being, and produces its reasonings from cause. According to the second definition, he calls dianoëtic knowledge science; but according to the first alone, he assigns to physiology the appellation of science.

The TELESTIC ART. The art pertaining to mystic ceremonies.

THEURGIC. This word is derived from θεουργια, or that religious operation which deifies him by whom it is performed as much as is possible to man.

TRUTH. Plato, following ancient theologists, considers truth multifariously. Hence, according to his doctrine, the highest truth is characterized by unity; and is the light proceeding from *The Good*, which imparts *purity*, as he says in the *Philebus*, and *union*, as he says in the *Republic*, to intelligibles. The truth which is next to this in dignity is that which proceeds from intelligibles, and illuminates the intellectual orders, and which an essence unfigured, uncoloured, and without contact, first receives, where also the plain of truth is situated, as it is written in the *Phædrus*. The third kind of truth is that which is connascent with souls, and which through intelligence comes into contact with true being. For the psychical light is the third from the intelligible; intellectual deriving its plenitude from intelligible light, and the psychical from the intellectual. And the last kind of truth is that which is in sensibles, which is full of error and inaccuracy through sense, and the instability of its object. For a material nature is perpetually flowing, and is not naturally adapted to abide even for a moment.

The following beautiful description of the third kind of truth, or that which subsists in souls, is given by Iamblichus: "Truth, as the name implies, makes a conversion about the gods and their incorporeal energy; but doxastic imitation, which, as Plato says, is fabricative of images, wanders about that which is deprived of divinity and is dark. And the former indeed receives its perfection in intelligible and divine forms, and real beings which have a perpetual sameness of subsistence; but the latter looks to that which is formless, and non-being, and which has a various subsistence; and about this its visive power is blunted. The former contemplates that which is; but the latter assumes such a form as appears to the many. Hence the former associates with intellect, and increases the intellectual nature which we contain; but the latter, from looking to that which always seems to be, hunts after folly and deceives." Iamblic. apud. Stob. p. 136.

The UNICAL. That which characterized by unity.

UNIFORM. This word when it occurs in Proclus, and other Platonic writers, signifies that which has the form of *The One*.

A WHOLE PRIOR TO PARTS. Whole has a triple subsistence. For it is either prior to parts; or it consists of parts; or it is in a part. The first of these is the cause of the parts it contains; just as a divine intellect is the cause of all the multitude of ideas it contains. The second is a whole *essentially*. And the third is a whole according to *participation*.

Index

Illustrations:

The Prometheus Trust

www.prometheustrust.co.uk

The Prometheus Trust exists to encourage, promote and assist the flowering of philosophy as the living love of wisdom; and is dedicated to the re-establishment of philosophy as the primary education of the human soul.

The Trust has an extensive and on-going publishing programme, at the heart of which is its Thomas Taylor Series: for details of our catalogue see overleaf.

Our education programme is based on the truth that philosophy is the *love of wisdom*: we welcome enquiries from any individual who is drawn to this affirmation, whether they be well established in the cultivation of philosophy or not. Our website is regularly updated with current details of our courses, as well as one-off workshops and public lectures.

The Trust has been running annual conferences in the UK since 2006 and is delighted by the wide range of participants and presenters, bringing together as they do highly regarded academics together with non-academics – the common ground being a determination to pursue philosophy as a guide to life. The Conference is usually planned for June or July, with its theme and call for papers issued in January – our website carries full details.

Also to be found on the website is our occasional web-journal, *The Meadow*, as well as recent news, several PDF files of interesting texts, and a page of inspiring thoughts drawn from the Platonic tradition, and much more besides.

The Prometheus Trust Catalogue

The Thomas Taylor Series

1 Proclus' Elements of Theology

Proclus' Elements of Theology - 211 propositions which frame the metaphysics of the Late Athenian Academy. 978-1898910-008

2 Select Works of Porphyry

Abstinence from Animal Food; Auxiliaries to the Perception of Intelligibles; Concerning Homer's Cave of the Nymphs; Taylor on the Wanderings of Ulysses. 978-1898910-015

3 Collected Writings of Plotinus

Twenty-seven treatises being all the writings of Plotinus translated by Taylor. 978-1898910-022

4 Writings on the Gods & the World

Sallust On the Gods & the World; Sentences of Demophilus; Ocellus on the Nature of the Universe; Taurus and Proclus on the Eternity of the World; Maternus on the Thema Mundi; The Emperor Julian's Orations to the Mother of Gods and to the Sovereign Sun; Synesius on Providence; Taylor's essays on the Mythology and the Theology of the Greeks. 978-1898910-039

5 Hymns and Initiations

The Hymns of Orpheus together with all the published hymns translated or written by Taylor; Taylor's 1824 essay on Orpheus (together with the 1787 version). 978-1898910-046

6 Dissertations of Maximus Tyrius

Forty-one treatises from the middle Platonist, and an essay from Taylor, The Triumph of the Wise Man over Fortune. 978-1898910-053

7 Oracles and Mysteries

A Collection of Chaldean Oracles; Essays on the Eleusinian and Bacchic Mysteries; The History of the Restoration of the Platonic Theology; On the Immortality of the Soul. 978-1898910-060

8 The Theology of Plato

The six books of Proclus on the Theology of Plato; to which is added a further book (by Taylor), replacing the original seventh book by Proclus, now lost. Extensive introduction and notes are also added. 978-1898910-077

9 Works of Plato I

Taylor's General Introduction, Life of Plato, First Alcibiades (with much of Proclus' Commentary), Republic (& extracts of Proclus' Scholia). 978-1898910-084

10 Works of Plato II

Laws, Epinomis, Timæus (with notes from Proclus' Commentary), Critias. 978-1898910-091

23 The Works of Aristotle V
The Metaphysics with notes from the Commentaries of Alexander Aphrodisiensis and Syrianus; Against the Dogmas of Xenophanes, Zeno and Gorgias; Mechanical Problems; On the World; On Virtues and Vices; On Audibles. 978-1898910-220

24 The Works of Aristotle VI
On the Soul (with much of the Commentary of Simplicius); On Sense and Sensibles; On Memory and Reminiscence; On Sleep and Wakefulness; On Dreams; On Divination by Sleep; On the Common Motions of Animals; On the Generation of Animals; On Length and Shortness of Life; On Youth and Old Age, Life and Death; On Respiration. 978-1898910-237

25 The Works of Aristotle VII
On the Heavens (with much of the Commentary of Simplicius); On Generation and Corruption; On Meteors (with much of the Commentary of Olympiodorus). 978-1898910-244

26 The Works of Aristotle VIII
History of Animals, & the Treatise on Physiognomy. 978-1898910-251

27 The Works of Aristotle IX
The Parts of Animals; The Progressive Motions of Animals, The Problems; On Indivisible Lines. 978-1898910-268

28 The Philosophy of Aristotle
Taylor's four part dissertation on the philosophy of Aristotle which outlines his primary teachings, the harmony of Plato and Aristotle, and modern misunderstandings of Aristotle. 978-1898910-275

29 Proclus' Commentary on Euclid
Proclus' Commentary on the First Book of Euclid's Elements; Taylor's four part Dissertation on the Platonic Doctrine of Ideas, on Demonstrative Syllogism, On the Nature of the Soul, and on the True End of Geometry. 978-1898910-282

30 The Theoretical Arithmetic of the Pythagoreans
The Theoretic Arithmetic of the Pythagoreans, Medicina Mentis, Nullities & Diverging Series, The Elements of a New Arithmetic Notation, Elements of True Arithmetic of Infinities. 978-1898910-299

31 & 32 Pausanias' Guide to Greece
Pausanias' Guide to Greece (in two volumes) with illustrations and extensive notes on mythology. 978-1898910-305 & 978-1898910-312

33 Against the Christians and Other Writings
The Arguments of Julian Against the Christians; Celsus, Porphyry and Julian Against the Christians; Writings of Thomas Taylor from his Collectanea, his Miscellanies in Prose and Verse, and his short works On Critics, An Answer to Dr Gillies, A Vindication of the Rights of Brutes, and his articles from the Classical Journal. Included is a Thomas Taylor bibliography. 978-1898910-32

Platonic Texts and Translations Series

Students' Edition Paperbacks

Music of Philosophy Series

Adapted by Guy Wyndham-Jones

A Casting of Light by the Platonic Tradition   978-1-898910-572

The Song of Proclus   978-1-898910-626

The Chant of Plotinus   978-1-898910-657

The Music of Plato   978-1-898910-671

The Hymn of Thomas Taylor   978-1-898910-688

A Flight of Souls   978-1-898910-695

Other titles available from the Prometheus Trust

Philosophy as a Rite of Rebirth – From Ancient Egypt to Neoplatonism
Algis Uždavinys   978-1898910-350

The Philosophy of Proclus – the Final Phase of Ancient Thought
L J Rosán   978-1898910-442

The Seven Myths of the Soul
Tim Addey   978-1898910-374

An Index to Plato
A Subject Index using Stephanus pagination. 978-1898910-343

Release Thyself – Three Philosophic Dialogues
Guy Wyndham-Jones   978-1-898910-565

Platonism and the World Crisis
John M Dillon, Brendan O'Byrne and Tim Addey   978-1-898910-5-8

Towards the Noosphere – Futures Singular and Plural
John M Dillon and Stephen R L Clark   978-1-898910-602

Metaphysical Patterns in Platonism
Edited by John F Finamore & Robert M Berchman   978-898910- 831

Song of the Solipsistic One
Deepa Majumdar   978-1-898910-633

Selections from the Prometheus Trust Confernces 2006-10
Edited by Linda Woodhouse   978-1-898910-66-4